PRAISE FOR
BE A WARRIOR IN BUSINESS

"Every leader needs to read *Be a Warrior in Business*. Rita and Nipendra have provided a blueprint for how to grow, sustain, and persevere in today's unpredictable business climate. This book is a game changer."

—JOHN R. DIJULIUS III, best-selling author of
The Customer Service Revolution

"*Be a Warrior in Business* delivers on its name by providing powerful strategies for building strong teams, cultivating winning cultures through operational excellence, and being ready for the unexpected. Whether you're an entrepreneur, CEO, or an up-and-coming leader, this is a must-read for anyone dedicated to pursuing—and achieving—lasting success."

—DUSTIN S. KLEIN, best-selling author
and veteran business journalist

"Planning for success in business draws many parallels to preparing for battle. In Rita and Nipendra Singh's cleverly written book, the authors capture the quintessential elements of leadership, team formation, decision-making, and mindset necessary to ensure success on the business battleground. This book is an excellent learning tool for those striving for success in business and a must-read for the business leaders of today and tomorrow."

—JOSEPH E. FRITZ, executive director,
Investment Casting Institute

"Based upon their extensive experience, Rita and Nipendra Singh have eloquently enumerated and described the behaviors and mindset to be a successful leader and entrepreneur. Anyone interested in maximizing their potential for success will benefit from this lucid, thought-provoking, and practical guide."

—DR. TOBY COSGROVE, former CEO, Cleveland Clinic

"Rita and Nipendra have had storied entrepreneurial journeys and have incredible insights and experiences to share. *Be a Warrior in Business* is a perfect demonstration of their continued commitment to building the small business community and helping leaders build strong teams and successful business ventures."

—MEGAN KIM, executive director,
Council of Smaller Enterprises (COSE)

"*Be a Warrior in Business* provides us with so many suggestions about how to enhance the peak performance, resilience, and integration of our organizations. This book is an immense help for leaders with visions for future growth."

—MITSUHIRO TAKEKAWA, senior associate director/division director,
Research and Engineering Division, Aero Engine,
Space and Defense Business Area, IHI Corporation

"The book *Be a Warrior in Business* is full of insightful and inspiring information on how to change your mindset on leading and running a business and how to lead through times of uncertainty."

—JOSEPH LAFLAMME, president, Vestshell Inc.

"A fast-paced and practical template to become savvy, strategic, and skilled in business and an inspiring, collaborative, and motivating team leader! Drawing on their compelling personal stories as successful business leaders themselves, Nipendra and Rita Singh powerfully guide us in how not just to survive, but succeed and thrive, in the world of business."

—DIANA BILIMORIA, PhD, KeyBank Professor, chair and professor of Organizational Behavior, Weatherhead School of Management, Case Western Reserve University

"The frame of small business owner as warrior is one that resonates with me. Toughness, preparation, commitment, decisiveness, and empathy are all traits that the best of the small business owners I have known exhibit every day. The mix of anecdotes, conventional wisdom and personal experience Rita and Nip share provide a reminder of the grit it takes to start, run, and grow a small business in the daily war for success."

—STEVE MILLARD, president and CEO, Greater Akron Chamber

"*Be a Warrior in Business* is a great handbook, guidebook, and how-to resource. It's filled with leadership gems as well as many examples, exercises, case studies, and step-by-step processes. Be prepared to reinvent yourself as you contemplate and put into action the down-to-earth, practical, and leadership-building wisdom found within its pages!"

—RATANJIT S. SONDHE, entrepreneur, author, and TV and radio host; founder, Discover Oneness Foundation

"Knowledge is power. This book gives you just that. With Rita and Nip's many years of experience, they have developed a comprehensive breakdown of not only how to be successful in business, but also how to be a great leader. It's perfect for a new entrepreneur just starting out or the owner of a thirty-seven-year-old business who still has many things to learn!"

—**JOE MINEO,** owner and creative director, Joe Mineo Creative

"Anyone seriously committed to proven role-model leadership needs to access this important volume today. *Be a Warrior in Business* will ignite your fighting spirit for your organization and for life!"

—**CAROL-ANN HAMILTON,** leadership author,
coach, and podcaster

"Rita and Nipendra skillfully translate the timeless wisdom of Vedanta into a business context, providing a guide not only for achieving success but, more importantly, for fostering spiritual growth."

—**ACHARYA VIVEK GUPTA,** spiritual teacher
and self-development guide, Chinmaya Mission
Niagara-Cleveland; speaker and author

"In today's rapidly changing business environment, where resilience and adaptability are more critical than ever, Rita and Nipendra' s insights will be invaluable to leaders looking to build strong, agile organizations that can thrive amid uncertainty. What sets the Singhs apart is not only their business acumen but also their unwavering commitment to ethics and empowering the communities around them, which has been the foundation of their own success."

—**DEEPAK TANDON,** senior partner and
development manager with world's
largest cloud service provider

"A riveting journey from start to finish, *Be a Warrior in Business* will empower you with the drive, determination, and strategy to become the leader of a team that can overcome any obstacle."

—**Y.K. SUD,** CA, director, Fibretech Leathers Private Limited

"*Be a Warrior in Business* is a testament of Rita and Nip's leadership journey. This book shares insights from their combined wealth of experience making it invaluable for all leaders—past, present and emerging."

—**KAVITA KASHYAP,** executive leader, strategist, and business transformation consultant

BE A
WARRIOR IN
BUSINESS

How to Develop
Resilient Organizations & Teams

RITA SINGH | NIPENDRA SINGH

RIVER GROVE
BOOKS

This publication is designed to provide accurate and authoritative information in regard to the subject matter covered. It is sold with the understanding that the publisher and author are not engaged in rendering legal, accounting, or other professional services. Nothing herein shall create an attorney-client relationship, and nothing herein shall constitute legal advice or a solicitation to offer legal advice. If legal advice or other expert assistance is required, the services of a competent professional should be sought.

Published by River Grove Books
Austin, TX
www.rivergrovebooks.com

Distributed by River Grove Books

Design and composition by Greenleaf Book Group
Cover design by Greenleaf Book Group and Adrian Morgan
Cover image used under license from © gremlin | iStockphoto

Publisher's Cataloging-in-Publication data is available.

Print: 978-1-63299-908-5

eBook: 978-1-63299-909-2

Hardcover: 978-1-63299-948-1

First Edition

For every reader who finds a piece of themselves
within these chapters
To those who are prepared to battle against all odds
Find the courage to move forward through life's struggles!
To excel and to achieve more than they could have
ever imagined
Willing to sacrifice for the greater good
And fights the good fight
To lift and lead others along the way.

———————

Victorious warriors win first and then go to war,
while defeated warriors go to war first and then seek to win.

—SUN TZU

———————

CONTENTS

INTRODUCTION

TO MAKE IT IN TODAY'S BUSINESS WORLD, it's no longer enough to just have an amazing product or service. The decisions we need to make for the sake of our employees, companies, assets, and reputations are becoming increasingly more complex and yet are critical to our survival and growth. The global business climate is changing faster than ever, and we're faced with new challenges every day. Whether you run your own organization or work alongside others, like it or not, you're being pushed and pulled from all sides and attacked from different directions. Business leadership has more to balance, juggle, and solve than ever before, and the problems confronting us are dauntingly intertwined. No business leader or any person is immune to the challenges that come our way. It is not about planning or casting a vision; it requires the drive, the action, and establishing strategy to get through these tough times. The battles are endless, from managing conflicts to building culture, navigating digital transformations to managing data security, retaining top talent to securing funding, coping with market competition and fluctuations to making decisions around expansion, working sustainably to guide our organizations through inflation and economic downturn.

We must also acknowledge that we live in a world of post-pandemic shutdowns, a reality that has disrupted previous business models and created massive blowouts in every industry. Additionally, climate disasters, wars between countries, and other unprecedented historical events have created ripple effects in the global economy, the long-term outcomes of which remain to be seen. The enormous scale of these crises and their impact has evoked feelings of uncertainty, stress, anxiety, and fear in business owners across the globe, in every industry.

How effectively we navigate through these challenges and capitalize on these opportunities will determine the outcome of our future. The only way to stand tall and stay strong through the onslaught is to conceptualize the obstacles that today's business leaders like you face as battles and, therefore, come to understand yourself as a warrior. You must recognize that the stakes are too high and the landscape too risky to continue to go into battle unarmed and unprepared. To work effectively, make the right decisions, and ensure you are ready for whatever comes next, you must be prepared to confront difficulties and find solutions at any moment. You need to cultivate the mental toughness and the strategic mind of a warrior to stay focused, resilient, and relevant. It's the only way to carry out the missions, win the war, and do it all for the benefit of those you work with and for.

POSITION YOURSELF TO NOT ONLY PERSEVERE BUT ALSO TO REMAIN UNBEATEN.

While it may seem harsh at first, thinking of yourself as a warrior in business is a positive reframing of your relationship to the challenges you face. Being a warrior means you work better and smarter, engage more powerfully and meaningfully with people, experience more satisfaction in what you do, and position yourself to not only persevere but also remain unbeaten. On a personal level, being a warrior in this sense means developing mental stamina, gaining self-confidence, building more time for what's important, and learning to elevate the situations around you. Once you've experienced this shift in perception, the next time you're faced with adversity—at any level, whether industry-wide, company-specific, or personal—you will know that you have the tools you'll need to be resilient.

There is no time more crucial to seek resilience and adopt the habits and mind of a business warrior. In fact, failing to do so may cause you to operate within the realm of mediocrity and limit your ability to succeed to your highest capabilities. This book offers you the tools you need to have a mindset that ensures you can win against the everyday battles you face. If you take this change of perception to heart and practice this warrior mindset in your business, you will be able to achieve a victory that lasts. It is your readiness, level of preparedness, and understanding of the challenges you'll encounter that will allow you to thrive in business and in your personal life. If applied judiciously, the insights in this book can also improve your aptitude for innovating, finding breakthrough ideas, and identifying new markets for your products and services.

When we started our business back in 1989, we had to define ourselves. We stepped into unknown territory, where we had minimal business experience, no resources, and no financial backing to lean on. We realized that while we may not have had years of experience, we were passionate, enthusiastic, and driven to succeed. This realization led us to challenge ourselves daily, learn new skills, and commit to positive outcomes. We thrived on challenge and constantly set goals for ourselves. Our people skills were a bonus to our business too. We always wanted to help other people, and we had the knowledge and determination to go the extra mile for our clients.

Not only did this make our business successful, but it allowed us to set out on a path to find solutions for other businesses to succeed as well. We were natural leaders with a vision to empower ourselves and others with our respective strengths. We were always looking for an opportunity to do better and achieve greatness by giving our **absolute best**.

We came to this insight and the realization of what it means to be a warrior in business early on in our journey. We started our company when Nip was transitioning from a corporate management career to consulting. Rita was a homemaker, a new graduate, and a licensed CPA with no work experience in consulting. There we were, just starting a new business, with no clients, no income, no financial support, and without much experience running a consulting business. **Being business warriors was our only choice.** We could not go back; we had to fight and find every conceivable way to succeed. That warrior spirit gave us the ability to withstand the challenges we have faced over the past thirty-plus years. As owners of a start-up company, we came to the understanding very quickly that the ultimate responsibility for developing and managing our enterprise was on us, and we could not sit back and wait for business to come to us.

Today's small businesses have access to technology, informed data, and resources that weren't available decades ago when we started out. We had to step out of our comfort zone to meet people, listen, and watch how others had done it. Learning new programs and software, building relationships, serving the community, and learning new skills became the norm in our household. Our nine-year-old daughter not only assembled our desks, but she also even created our first business brochure on our computer at home. In this process of being out there in the field, we found mentors, coaches, new talent, resources, and answers to many of our clients' problems. Nip constantly traveled to far areas of North America and the rest of the world to meet with prospective clients, and that resulted in Nip becoming the go-to person in the manufacturing world of aerospace and other high-value components.

Rita, who engaged with both her professional and civic communities, became a trusted business advisor and coach. We constantly researched ways to assist clients, not only to keep the company competitive and profitable but also to have the ability to withstand the challenges that came our way due to market fluctuations. We sacrificed some of our needs, but we never lost sight of our goals.

As time went by, we evolved and our consulting areas grew. Our current consulting offerings are allocated into two primary areas: manufacturing technology and business management. The manufacturing technology branch, headed by Nip, focuses primarily on industry-specific consulting, investment casting, product/process development, scrap/cost reduction, market/technology research, strategy and innovation, and greenfield/brownfield projects in the metal and ceramic industries, mainly in the investment casting industry. The business management consulting branch, headed by Rita, works with individuals and businesses and their executives, focusing on understanding their goals and needs and identifying problems and solutions in the key areas of financial management; entrepreneurship and leadership development; strategic planning; diversity, equity, and inclusion; and human resources.

This book takes you on a journey that will increase your awareness, uplift your thought processes, and help you lead like a warrior by embracing the warrior's character, drive, and strategy. Along the way, you will see what kinds of obstacles leaders face, why being resilient is the key to overcoming them, and how to be and stay successful for the long term. You'll specifically learn what a warrior looks like in business and how resilience creates sustainability and fuels growth. From this, you and your teams will also be able to recognize how to better identify and address problems that always seem to come back to haunt you and your organization.

Each chapter of this book focuses on important attributes possessed by a business warrior. To overcome adversity and win your everyday battles, you'll first need to know how to think about and apply these qualities. Once you've learned them, you can go into battle with the right mindset, allowing you to lead like an everyday business warrior.

CHAPTER 1

A WARRIOR IN BUSINESS IS PREPARED FOR BATTLE

PREPARATION IS KEY FOR A WARRIOR IN business to emerge victorious. A seasoned warrior, when arriving at the scene of a battle, would not charge toward the action without first assessing the situation. They would first gauge the fight before them, identify the capabilities of their enemies, and then ensure they had the right equipment, protective gear, and troop support to enter the fray. It's no different in business. One of the best things you can do to alter and influence the outcome of a challenge is to prepare.

In the same way the odds would be stacked against an unprepared, uninformed warrior, you, too, will face heavy losses—even all-out defeat—if you run straight at a business problem without being ready. With the right preparation, you have the ability to affect what happens and how you and your organization go through the situation.

WHAT BATTLE PREPAREDNESS LOOKS LIKE

Benjamin Franklin once said, "By failing to prepare, you are preparing to fail." Preparedness means being proactive and wise, understanding what kind of situation you're entering before you go. To succeed, you must know where you're going, what you're going to face, what your goals are, and what you need to do to accomplish those goals. Preparedness gives you the information and tools you need to bring about an acceptable outcome. If you want to survive, you can't afford not to prepare.

Unfortunately, many people who start a business don't do enough preparation up front. Eager to get going, they march onto the battlefield, thinking they know enough. They advance confidently enough for a time but then suddenly find themselves in the thick of battle. Sometimes they struggle because they didn't get the lay of the land beforehand, didn't understand their competition, or didn't have the necessary resources to sustain a high level of performance in battle. As reported by the U.S. Small Business Administration, ". . . Over 50 percent of small businesses fail in the first year, and 95 percent fail within the first five years."[1] The fact is, they could have increased their chances of survival if they'd set themselves up for success in advance.

----

1   Moya K. Mason, "What Causes Small Businesses to Fail?" MKM Research, https://www.moyak.com/papers/small-business-failure.html#:~:text=Starting%20 a%20small%20business%20is,within%20the%20first%20five%20years.

Put Together a Good Business Plan

As seasoned consultants and business coaches, our advice for small and midsize business owners just starting out has always been to ensure that, at a bare minimum, they first have a good business plan. This allows them to plot their course before proceeding, so they can properly focus their efforts and have an effective strategy for growth. Whether you're in a hundred-thousand-dollar business or a hundred-million-dollar business, starting out new or already in operation for several years, a good business plan is critical. A business plan ensures you have the fundamental elements in place before you launch or take the next step in growth. It shows your employees, investors, and partners that you are serious, thoughtful, and driven when it comes to your business and where you'd like to take it. This has the secondary benefit of building trust with your key stakeholders, showing them what they can expect from you, and encouraging them to be involved.

It is possible to fly by the seat of your pants and rely on your personal strengths to get you through, and there are many historical anecdotes that might support taking that approach. But considering that so much is unpredictable in business, we don't recommend it. Why make yourself vulnerable to challenges or set yourself up for defeat? We've been in business for thirty-five years in part because we have continuously prepared and *always* kept an eye on our business plan as we grew and made decisions around how to best serve our clients.

Ideally, your business plan will be complete before you launch. Then, from launch to scaling, you will need to consistently assess the plan while measuring performance, making sure it is aligned with your goals. A business plan should include all the necessary pieces for your organization's viability, especially the following:

- **Financial plan**—Estimate, to the best of your ability with all the information at your disposal, your future or ongoing financial needs.

- **Management plan** (a.k.a. "the **people plan**")—Decide who is going to lead and manage the business. This plan should also lay out how to empower your employees, equipping them with the tools and resources they need to feel confident going out into the world to make the organization successful.

- **Marketing plan**—Really get to know your market, your competition, and your client/consumer so you can strategically position your brand.

- **Operational plan**—Detail your step-by-step approach to managing the everyday activities of your business and plot the concrete steps required to take your organization to the next level of growth.

The time you invest in your business plan now will reduce your risk of pursuing the wrong opportunity or wasting resources. You'll not only have a sound plan for weathering ups and downs, giving your employees a clear vision of where they're heading, but you'll also have the knowledge to rivet back in the face of any challenges or fluctuations that may occur in the future. A high level of preparedness allows for resiliency by enabling you to reposition your business effectively with changing conditions. Companies that are prepared also have the courage to take some calculated risks. When you have a plan in place, you make your business more attractive to investors, creditors, and lenders. With preparation, you are making a clear pathway for yourself, your organization, and your investors.

WHEN YOU HAVE A PLAN IN PLACE, YOU MAKE YOUR BUSINESS MORE ATTRACTIVE TO INVESTORS, CREDITORS, AND LENDERS.

Think for a moment about what would happen if you were hit by a truck but had no contingency plan figured out in advance. What would happen to your business or to your family? If the injuries are severe enough or the recovery time too long, you could stand to lose everything. Situations like losing a business partner, key employee, or family member—or even facing a serious health condition yourself—can cause great hardship. With advance preparation, you will be able to get through the storms and hardships better. You can be preemptive and respond with a plan in place rather than react in the moment when you may not have your wits about you.

If you have a solid business plan in place, even if you need to continue to tweak and adjust parts of it, you'll be setting yourself up for success. It can and should be a work in progress, changing as you revisit it periodically. It doesn't have to be a hundred pages long, either; it could be as simple as one to four pages. Do whatever works best for you and makes sense for your business. You'll feel less stressed and be more ready, knowing you have the fundamentals in place.

Know What Kind of Battle You're Entering

Before you know the best action to take in battle, you must know what you're getting into. What kind of space are you entering? Who are the competitors? If you don't know what's ahead, you could risk damaging your organization's credibility and reputation. Preparing for the battle to come involves doing advance research, talking to key stakeholders, and building your knowledge so you understand the context and situation. This is what makes a business warrior tactically proficient, so they're always ready with what they need to fight, increasing their odds of success.

Think about what you will face, get the lay of the land, take stock of your resources, and imagine how you're going to get your business across the battlefield safely to the other side. Think ahead about the battle beyond the present battle. A war is made up of more than one fight. It involves strategy and a broad perspective if you are to survive. At the end, rather than just remaining standing, you want to be victorious, known as a top contender in your space.

Preparedness enables you to understand the big picture more fully but also in a granular way. You can look at a situation from thirty thousand feet but also at twenty thousand feet and five thousand feet. The bird's-eye view provides one angle, but close-ups are crucial too. When a warrior enters combat, there isn't always much time to strategize. Going into a situation with a micro and macro understanding of what you face allows you to proceed with more confidence. Military operations deal with both the war as a whole and the people on the ground who are engaged in the action. In business, you also need to consider both.

Preparedness Case Study: S&A Consulting Group

We didn't enter our consulting business simply because it was what we wanted to do, hoping that by some stroke of luck it would work out. We were intentional as we built our business; the secret to our success involved a lot of advance preparation. But now, many such practices have become a part of everyday life for us. The following are some of the specific actions we took when we were getting our business off the ground. Each of these efforts was essential in helping us develop relationships, build trust, and gain experience in our chosen field.

- We took the time to research our prospective clients—who they were, what kept them up at night, what they needed, what challenges they faced, what problems or pain points drove them crazy, and why our business would not only provide immediate solutions but also serve as a good resource for them in the long term.
- We volunteered and served in various business and civic organizations and shared our time and talents with others, without any expectations.
- We attended many business conferences, forums, and networking events to collaborate with other organizations and to gain knowledge about new industry trends.

- We mentored other business professionals and at the same time sought mentors in and outside our industry to learn from their experiences.
- All of the above paid off. We developed our knowledge base, resources, and relationships, and our business grew exponentially. Preparedness enabled us to act quickly and decisively, allowing us to recognize, seize, and capitalize on opportunities when they occurred. It made us proactive in taking steps to ensure that we were ready for whatever came our way.
- While our client base grew, we discovered diverse talent that could support our projects. We started getting referrals from clients and organizations where we served. And our business took off. Our work gained notice for the value we brought to our clients. Nip was recognized by the investment casting industry and inducted into the Hall of Honor. Rita received a lot of recognition and numerous awards from the business community, including Small Business Administration (SBA) Accountant Advocate of the Year, SBA Northern Ohio Women in Business Champion of the Year, Businesswoman of the Year from the Business Advisory Council of the National Republican Congressional Committee, Enterprising Women of the Year from *Enterprising Women* magazine, and induction into the Ohio Women's Hall of Fame. And S&A as a company was recognized many times by *Smart Business* as an honoree of their World-Class Customer Service Award.

Prepare for Entry

On your path to success in business, many variables will affect your experience. The following are some timeless strategies for adequately preparing yourself to enter the market space you have chosen. Some of the preparation mentioned here will depend on the nature of your business, what industry you are operating in, and whether you are a start-up or an existing business.

- Business comes from the community. When we make our mission to engage and serve others, without any expectations, the end results are

continued

phenomenal. Through alliances, strategic partnerships, and relationships, you can develop many resources for your business, whether your objective is to find the right talent for a project, obtain a mentor, or discover new opportunities. Being visible in the community will not only bring you more business but will also create long-lasting relationships. It is an investment of your time, but the return is worth it.

- Narrow down and determine who you want to be your customer. Know how to identify your client base. Trying to be everything to everyone is not a good approach. Concentrating your focus will help reduce stress. You can't please everyone, but once you figure out who your target customer is, you've found your niche. Then you can focus on delivering the products or services that your real audience gets excited about.

- Learn new skills on how to research and market your product or service.

- Take professional development courses that focus on financial management, operations, marketing, weathering trends, growing your business, investing in your people, and so on.

- Participate in business forums and conferences to gain new knowledge and trends in your specific industry.

- Be a mentee and a mentor.

- Every industry has an association that can serve as a rich source of business information. Join professional organizations to connect with other business owners and suppliers, find mentors, and obtain information on discounts, health insurance, and workers' compensation.

- Identify the research and training you will need to face the challenges common in your market space and among your competitors. Gather data about the products, sales, and marketing strategies of your competitors (i.e., other businesses in the same industry or providing similar or the same services). This data can be used to identify your strengths and weaknesses and help you discover potential opportunities. This competitive analysis can help you understand the market landscape and make informed decisions to improve your position.

Back when we first started, the research we needed to adequately prepare ourselves was much harder to come by than it is today. We had to physically call people—on landline telephones—to get the information and resources we needed. And just like starting out with any new business, the information we needed was both internal and external. Internal insight included information about employees, subcontractors, sales, and customers. External information pertained to the industry, the competition, and governmental regulations. Gathering this kind of data is much easier now than it was back then!

At the time, we needed to do all our own legwork up front. We soon found that starting or building a business is like giving birth and then nurturing, developing, and raising a newborn from childhood to adulthood. When you are a sole proprietor, you are like a single mom or dad trying to do the job of both, performing multiple tasks—building relationships with clients, developing and improving your roster of products and services, cutting costs, and sometimes even serving as your own IT and HR departments. When you try to perform all these tasks at the same time, your business becomes very demanding. Wearing so many hats can actually slow down the growth of your business.

How can you solve this overload? You will need to farm out the legwork, delegating the right functions to the right people, to speed up the growth of your business. Your support network can be made up of many kinds of people. Think of hiring someone or an on-call basis, such as an IT consultant or an accountant to do your books, or outsourcing payroll functions to a payroll company. Build a supportive network with insurance consultants, lawyers, and suppliers who will keep your business moving forward and will afford you more time to think things through. For our business, we hired a bookkeeper and administrative assistant to answer our calls, conduct research, track projects, manage expenses, and do our billing and invoices on a timely basis. We retained a travel agency, which we use to this day, to take care of our travel arrangements within or outside the country.

PREPARATION MOSTLY TAKES PLACE DURING TIMES OF PEACE.

Preparation also allows you to reposition your organization when you need to adapt to changing conditions over time. You will not only have a sound plan in cases of economic downturns or other global factors but also in cases of unexpected trends in your industry, changes in technology, or evolving customer needs. This is how you stay resilient as a small-to-mid-size business in today's competitive environment. Business warriors never wait for the war to start before they train for future challenges. Preparation, including learning new skills through training, mostly takes place during times of peace.

Focus on What's Most Important

A business warrior knows they can't control everything, but they can control themselves and their responses. To that end, they are focused and fully engaged in what they can control. They don't answer unnecessary chats or video calls in meetings, because they know they're in combat and need to stay alert to catch all the details and respond accordingly—they can't afford not to, because the cost is great. If you want to be ready to act and to survive, 100 percent of your mental commitment is required. Business warriors count the costs and prioritize, knowing it's okay to be unreachable at times, for the greater good. They won't make it in battle if they're distracted or focused on the wrong things.

When we first visualized starting our own small business, it was a time when Nip was constantly traveling for work and Rita was busily preparing for her CPA exam while caring for their young children. She was loaded up with school activities, homework assistance, and household management. As a warrior in business, she recognized that this was a season in which she needed to focus on what was needed most, which meant she had to sacrifice some things such as regular meetings with friends and other activities. She made that choice because she knew that for the greater good, this was the action she needed to take to prepare. She devoted herself to these pursuits for three to four years to ensure she was able to do what she needed to do well. It was a tough, all-consuming time, but because she knew this was part of the necessary preparation, she didn't give up and stayed up well past midnight most nights to accomplish the necessary tasks. Shortly after receiving her CPA designation, she and Nip launched S&A Consulting Group.

THINK ABOUT WHAT YOU WANT TO BE ABOUT

Ask yourself

- Why am I in business?
- What is the purpose?
- What are my short-term goals?
- What are my long-term goals?
- Is my business model sustainable?
- Is my product or service needed in the marketplace?

Any small business owner or person in a leadership position, whether they're just getting started or have been in business for a while, needs to ask these questions. They can always be doing things better, and it's never too late to make a change. Taking this kind of inventory will help you move forward and know how to operate to reach your goals. You don't want to try all sorts of things on the battlefield while not really knowing what you're there to fight for; the risk is too great.

A warrior in business knows who they are and what they want to embody. Before you choose to go into battle, make sure that your chosen direction is aligned with your goals and who you are. In business, it is so important to know your purpose. Are you there to sell a product or a service, to make money to be profitable, or to create a name for yourself? Do you want to serve the community and make a difference, changing the world for the better? Do you feel you have a social responsibility above and beyond your products and services? What can you do outside your work and home life to help others? Think qualitatively about what it is that you do and stand for. What is the purpose and ultimate goal of your business? Before you start your venture, be very clear about what you want out of it. Take inventory of yourself on a business level. A soldier protects and safeguards their country and comrades. There is a deeper meaning behind their actions, which is to serve others during peace, conflict, or war. In business, if your focus is to *serve*, then it changes the whole dynamic around what you do because you are putting people above profits and serving humanity through your products and services.

Hone Your Skills

Your level of education, past successes, and passion are not always enough to get you through adversity or help you win the battle. You can rest on those laurels for a time, but winning takes more. If you have a lot of military training, it doesn't mean anything if you go into battle and then just stand there. To make it in business, you need to be ready for what's to come and willing to act accordingly. Preparation includes learning new skills and building on old ones, updating your knowledge, and checking your understanding.

You must continually engage in this process, whatever the nature of your business. If you need to research, learn a new technology, gain more education, or become part of a larger network, you must be continually connected in that action. You're trained in your field or have the knowledge relevant to your industry, but to be ready for the unexpected, make sure your training isn't based on yesterday's knowledge. Every minute, things change. When you stay invested in learning and growing, it allows you to stay relevant and present. And those are qualities that are necessary for long-term resilience in business.

Many professional associations require you to build your skills and knowledge every year or take some courses to better understand recent changes. It is imperative for business owners to remain competitive. Investing in employee training and development improves productivity and secures the company's future, even in the most aggressive industries. You must always find ways to continuously sharpen your skills and to develop your mindset.

As part of continuous learning, there are active things you can do. One of those is to pursue professional development opportunities—to constantly read, research, bridge the gaps, or fill the holes—to add to your skill set, especially in today's rapidly shifting landscape. As technology changes, you will not be able to stay resilient unless you can use and leverage the technology effectively. So, it's important to empower yourself with education and knowledge by learning new technologies and nurturing an environment conducive to your mental growth, which will enable you to bring innovation, new ideas, and solutions to your clients and customers.

If you're going up a ladder with a screwdriver in hand to accomplish a task, you don't want to get to the top of the ladder just to discover you also need a hammer. You'll have to go back down the ladder to get a hammer before you can get the job done. Prepare and think about what you need beforehand so you can save time and be better equipped. Go up the ladder with what you need. The more tools in your tool belt, the better prepared you are for doing the job properly and punctually. In business, you need to look up the ladder and at the task at hand to first determine what tools, knowledge, and training are required, or if you need to enlist the help of another. You don't want to be at the top of the ladder in a treacherous position, accomplishing nothing and wondering what to do and how to do it.

Build Your Resources and Talent Base

When we look at our own organization, we know that without financial and people resources, we would not have been able to do business worldwide. Period. A resource is any factor that's necessary to accomplish a goal or conduct an activity to manage business. In today's economy, a successful business must understand the resources it needs, how those resources support the business model, and how to make the most of them. Every business has its own unique needs, of course, but some common types of resources are labor, equipment, finances, time, and energy. One key example is financial resources. Having a line of credit and securing the capital to fund your business are critical lifelines so a business has cash flow and the financial backing to pay for obligations such as employees, rent, utilities, loans, and so on. We found empowerment by finding the right talent. Once a small company like ours finds the right talent, it can take on any type of project. In our case, we were able to take on various projects in multiple locations not just because of the two of us, but also because of the additional pool of talented consultants we had brought to our team. That's the message we are giving to those small companies: You have the ability to do anything, anywhere you want to, if you have the right talent.

Invest in Sharpening Your Axe

Abraham Lincoln once said, "If I had eight hours to chop down a tree, I'd spend six hours sharpening my axe." You have already learned why preparation is a good idea, but why do we not do this enough, or sometimes even skip this crucial step? For most of us, it is hard to follow a regimen, adhere to an effective routine, and practice discipline on a daily basis. But warriors must prepare themselves both physically and mentally. That is how they develop the kind of physical and mental toughness needed for breakthrough success in their own field of battle.

Being prepared takes effort, discipline, and investment. To be resilient in business and war, start by making preparation a habit and build healthy practices to support it. We believe all good business warriors develop and follow a routine. Preparation and practice can become second nature to you, an integral part of how you think and act. You've probably heard or read about "the Spartan way." For the Spartans, courage was not "a vulnerable and transitory state of mind, but the product of preparation and practice. The courage of the Spartans was not born of feeling, but discipline. And it was not an emotion, but a habit."[2]

The business warrior is similarly disciplined. Daily, they go through a tough regimen and rituals, preparing their bodies and minds to succeed under any circumstances. The first thing they do is keep their bodies fit through vigorous exercise. But it is not enough to just work on the body alone. The mind must be equally fierce, full, and ready; mental muscle and determination are a must. A strong mind can make up for a weak body, but a strong body cannot make up for a weak mind.

A warrior in business develops a keen sense of self-awareness. Businesses should review their situation from time to time—at least once a year—on SWOT (strengths, weaknesses, opportunities, and threats). What do you do well? What could you improve? What opportunities are open to you? What threats could impair you? SWOT analysis can help you evaluate what your company does best now and prepare a successful strategy for the future. SWOT analysis looks at both internal and external factors. Some may be in your control, and some will be out of your control. The importance of SWOT analysis is that it uncovers threatening blind spots about your organization's performance. SWOT can deliver new insights into where your business currently is. You may discover some

----

2   Brett and Kate McKay, "The Spartan Way: The Mindset and Tactics of a Battle-Ready Warrior," *The Strenuous Life* (blog), updated July 1, 2023, https://www.artofmanliness.com/character/military/the-spartan-way-the-mindset-and-tactics-of-a-battle-ready-warrior/.

opportunities, and it will help you develop the right strategy for any situation. Although you can perform an informal SWOT analysis, for a more effective SWOT analysis, we recommend that you hire an external coach or use the resources available to you within your organization.

A business warrior never stops building their skills and developing themselves. The more difficult a situation, the more rigorously they prepare. They're open to growing, improving, and doing what it takes to get better. They recognize that even as the business climate rapidly changes, they themselves are also a work in progress, adding to their skill set and personal toolbox all the time. Once you've equipped yourself with the skills, training, and discipline you need, you'll be ready to take action.

BE READY FOR THE EXPECTED BUT ALSO THE UNEXPECTED

Business warriors do not wait for the war to start before getting themselves trained and prepared. Ideally, you have the chance to prepare during times of peace—that is, outside of battle, when things are going well for your business, your clients aren't experiencing any crises, your internal teams are functioning healthily, and the economy is doing well. Because once the unexpected happens, you need to be in position, poised for action. Without action, nothing happens, even if you've done the best planning. Theories and ideas are great, but without getting up and executing, nothing will happen.

If you leave water in a glass for a week, it isn't fresh anymore. In fact, it stagnates. But running water has energy and forward motion. It's fresh, it's going somewhere, it's not stuck in one place doing nothing. Anyone who wants to be successful in business must move forward. They can't just stand in one place—they need to prepare to advance and to take action.

To be an effective, resilient leader who can overcome adversity, it's important not to get stuck without realizing it. Success is not a given, so you should always be fluid in your approach. You should always be growing and staying in tune with what you see happening—whatever that landscape, that battle, or that challenge looks like. Learn, adapt, and deliver at the highest caliber you can at any given time. Preparation is a skill you can learn. It's not in your DNA or something you get from your parents. If your goal is to be prepared and resilient, you must continue sharpening your skills and remain an ongoing learner. You have to sharpen your axe.

You will always be faced with unknown and untried situations in business. Circumstances in the world change. Other businesses don't always play by the rules (or they play by a different set!). Preparedness is one of the first steps before any battle and will give you a mental edge, so you are prepared to manage challenges, find solutions to problems, and better bounce back from unexpected issues.

Preparing for unpredicted problems or crises doesn't have to be negative. Focus rather on what sets you up for success. On an airplane, with the understanding you may encounter turbulence, you simply wear a seat belt but otherwise continue enjoying your flight. If there's an emergency, you're already doing what you need to be doing and can then apply further measures. Preparedness allows you to have greater control over your decisions and the actions you choose to take. Manage what you can now, planning for the good and better times later. It's a good everyday business practice to always look ahead and find ways to prepare yourself. This will contribute to your success, which allows you to achieve resilience.

We mention earlier that the best time to prepare is in periods of peace, when we have the time and energy for it. You can think with a clearer mind, put precautions in place, and train your people. And when what goes up comes down—because it always does; change is inevitable—everyone is ready. If there's a downturn in the economy, the businesses that have prepared don't always have to lay off people, because they were preemptive, armed with a contingency plan, and ready for growth.

As a business warrior, besides being poised for action, informed, and mentally prepared to make sound decisions, you should also be intuitive and observant. This means gaining and maintaining situational awareness. With this understanding, you will be better equipped to choose the right interactions in their environment—a critical element in making sound decisions. Preparedness allows you to think clearly now so you can be intentional tomorrow.

As reported in the *Wall Street Journal* and other financial publications in 2008 and 2009, General Motors and Chrysler ran out of cash and needed taxpayer bailouts to avoid bankruptcy. This is where Ford Motor Company's advance planning paid off. Prior to the credit crunch, Ford began to restructure its debt and raised billions as it continually added to its cash reserves. The company understood the importance of advance planning to prepare for what might lie ahead.

As you prepare for battle, take special note of holes or areas of weakness and look for the right ways to fill them. If you know about a hole but don't do anything about it, you leave yourself vulnerable during battle. This leaves you unprepared and prone to arriving at an outcome you don't want. With the awareness you glean from your advanced preparedness, you can determine your outcome better.

Most important, you must also know that all the preparation you do *still* won't prepare you for absolutely everything. Prepare, prepare, prepare, but don't be surprised if all the measures you take don't get you through every circumstance. Preparation, however, increases your opportunity for success. A good, effective leader needs to be ready but also flexible in their thinking, willing to adjust their expectations, and able to alter the resulting actions accordingly.

ENGAGE OTHERS

In the preparation stage, it's always helpful to engage another professional or specialist to help. In areas where we may be weak or don't have all the information we need, we can't always solve problems by ourselves. Asking for external help or soliciting feedback and information from others goes a long way toward getting us prepared in certain circumstances. Reach out for mentoring, coaching, or guidance if you need it. Learn from those who've walked the steps before you. Listen to those who have expertise to share. As capable as you may be, you need to engage other people if you want to be resilient.

NO ONE CAN DO IT ALONE.

With all the work that goes into launching, running, and sustaining your business, you won't be able to do it all alone. During the COVID-19 pandemic, we consistently found that people who had strong interpersonal relationships with others were more resilient. No one can do it alone. The smart move is to align yourself with people you can lean on. And in turn, do this for others who need you too.

What we're suggesting is the difference between short-term thinking and long-term thinking. If, for example, you know you need to enlist the help of an expert, yet you feel you can't afford it, this could cost you in the long run. To be resilient in business, you must think down the road and prepare yourself for what you need. Invest in yourself and your business up front so you can make it through the battle ahead. In our early years of business, we could barely afford to attend industry conferences. It was a lot of money to us at the time, but we knew we needed to invest in that. Nip showed his face year after year at the relevant conferences, built connections, tapped into resources, and established his reputation as an expert. Rita recognized the benefits of professional relationships and the need to build her reputation and credibility as well. This willingness to connect with others served us well in the long run, and we still maintain and rely on some of those business relationships today.

For us, relationship-building has been key to our success. The partnerships, alliances, and resources we've developed have made us effective and relevant inside and outside our industry. Relationships are so critical, especially for small businesses where resources are limited. Early on, we struggled with building a client base, having a limited income and not knowing exactly what to do next. But we did know we needed to serve other people—finding meaningful, relevant ways to engage and participating in various professional civic organizations. That kind of exposure and connection gave us a chance to promote our competencies and shine. We nurtured those relationships over the years, and that's how business kept on coming back to us. We feel the biggest asset we have as a small company, then and now, is our ability to grow and serve through genuine relationships—giving back, developing partnerships, and establishing a meeting of minds, alliances, and experiences. We engage constantly on a personal level and a professional level.

So, part of all this is building relationships. If you want to be resilient and effective, you should always be open to, searching for, and nurturing genuine relationships. And often those become strategic relationships, good friendships, and good partnerships. This is necessary to remain relevant and engaged. Since our business purpose is to serve people, our interactions are not just simply social—they actually serve our business, influence our surroundings, and enhance our work dynamic.

Dwight D. Eisenhower once said, "In preparing for battle I have always found that plans are useless, but planning is indispensable." Think of preparation as a work in process. Before you advance or move forward, you must prepare. Preparation is one of the key character traits of a warrior in business and contributes directly to their ability to emerge as victorious.

THE WAY YOU THINK WILL AFFECT THE WAY YOU ACT.

If you want to overcome adversity, position yourself by being prepared with what you need to confront it. Keep in mind, the way you think will affect the way you act. The intentional preparation you do today will help you take care of tomorrow. Even when the battle isn't going your way, your advance preparation gives you the ability to cope better, provides you with needed insights that can help you repair a situation, restores confidence when you think you've lost it, and enables you to bounce back from other life challenges. Preparation empowers you to win on all fronts, allowing you to operate at your highest potential.

Executive Summary

- Preparation is one of the key traits of a warrior. **Preparation sets you up** for the outcome you want. The preparation we do today giving our absolute best will demonstrate our resilience and spirit of strength.

- Creating a **sound business plan** is the most essential form of preparation—for both new and established businesses.

- A good **business plan** includes the following elements:
    - **Financial plan**—future and ongoing financial needs
    - **Management plan**—who is going to lead and manage the business
    - **Marketing plan**—market, client/consumer, and competition research; brand positioning strategy
    - **Operational plan**—a detailed, step-by-step plan for managing the everyday activities of the business; detailed plans for future growth

- **Getting to know your market space and competitors** is a key part of preparing your business for success.

- **Examine your priorities** to ensure they are worthy of your time and focus. This allows you to devote yourself entirely to your goals.

- Preparation includes **learning new skills and building on old ones**, updating your knowledge, and checking your understanding.

- All good business warriors develop and follow a **routine**.

- **Preparation happens during times of peace.** Do not wait until you are facing the next challenge to prepare for it.

- All the preparation in the world still won't prepare you for everything. It will only **increase your opportunity for success**.

- Ask for help in areas you may be weak. Solicit feedback from peers. **Building relationships** with others will make you more resilient.

CHAPTER 2

A WARRIOR IN BUSINESS GOES ALL IN

To SUCCEED IN BUSINESS, YOU NEED TO be fully committed and personally invested. This requires taking ownership of all aspects of your business and yourself, holding yourself accountable for doing what is necessary and giving your absolute best. It demands that you focus on the right things and know how to turn your plans into the kind of action that gets the results you want.

You must be willing to lead the charge and see it through. A warrior in business looks out for their team and approaches the mission with everything they've got. They know it will call for ingenuity, quick thinking, stamina, peak performance, and sacrifice. They seek to gain ground and advance their initiatives. They know they have an objective they must accomplish, and that they will have to outlast and outperform their opponents. When they are victorious on the other side, they establish a reputation for themselves that makes other people take notice. Others may want to align themselves with the business warrior or seek them out for help.

Going all in with your small business isn't about having the right state of mind—although that's where it starts—it's a series of habits and best practices that allow you to face not just the everyday battles but also to engage in battle in a way that wins the war.

So, how does a warrior in business go all in?

FOCUS ON TODAY TO ACCOMPLISH THE MISSION

To go all in, you need to know what your objectives are. A warrior in business is clear on what the primary goal is and stays focused on that, never losing sight of it. As conditions, opponents, tools, and communications change, you still need to stay laser focused on your goal. Otherwise, you could lose your way and veer off course, causing you to miss your mark. Focus means thinking about the most important things while also filtering out other distractions. It's not that some of these distractions might not be important; instead, it's knowing how to prioritize where your attention is needed most.

If you keep your primary business goal in mind, you'll know how to move forward. Knowing your priorities will also help you determine how to invest your energy and attention in key decision-making, individual projects, and relationship-building strategies along the way.

When we talk about focus, we don't mean a single-minded preoccupation with the outcome or end result. In the *Bhagavad Gita*, a Hindu scripture, Shri Krishna teaches that for each of us, our responsibility is for our actions in the present *only*, not for the fruits those actions may reap in the *future*. To be a warrior in business, you must realize that in any given situation, you cannot do anything more than your best. You may have a desired outcome, but the actions you take and processes you follow are all you can take responsibility for in the present to work toward that outcome. Focusing only on the end result in business can breed a lot of anxiety. It can feel overwhelming and stressful. If you bring your focus closer to the present, without forgetting your desired outcome, you can concentrate your efforts on the process and your actions. This reduces those feelings of weakness and allows you to empower yourself through action.

Your success cannot be contingent on just attaining a particular result or outcome. Instead, it's helpful to look at success as a journey. It's not a destination but a holistic experience that can be full of meaning and joy. If you remove the overemphasis on success or failure, you become more able to give your best to the moment you're in now. Rather than being frozen by the pressure of thinking only about the future and intangible results, you will be able to deal with what's real now and see the actions you can take today to achieve your goal in the future. You can look at today's responsibilities and plans in the context of your larger business objectives and do something about them in the present.

The pressure to achieve results can create discontent and disillusionment. There's no point in approaching your future like that. Instead, eliminate the noise and distractions—focus on thinking about the next thing, then the next thing after that. Take one step forward at a time and do not worry more than you need to about pleasing others and satisfying the external factors. Rather, enjoy and learn from the experience as you go. Clear your mind of distractions to gain better control of today's tasks. If you can keep doing this, you can achieve the end result you want. Focus on the *process* you're undertaking or the moment you're in, so you can have better control of yourself today. In the long run, it's about conquering yourself, dedicating yourself to the process, and giving your best. The quality of the effort you put in is what matters.

A WARRIOR IN BUSINESS MUST KNOW HOW TO KEEP THEIR FOCUS ON THE RIGHT THING IN THE MOMENT.

A warrior in battle always knows their highest objective, but in the moment, they must keep their eyes on what's immediately around them. They need to stay present, attuned to whatever is in their vicinity and what they can see in their periphery. They need to think fast and take action based on the circumstances at hand, rather than being overly fixated on the future. If they're focused too far ahead, they could jeopardize the day's mission, endanger a fellow soldier's life, or give the other side an advantage. In much the same way, a warrior in business must know how to keep their focus on the right thing in the moment. They can't have tunnel vision or keep their eyes trained on the horizon if there are circumstances around them that they must manage now.

Establish Your Narrow and Wide Focuses

When you look through the lens of a single-lens reflex camera, you can focus it in different ways. There are wide- and narrow-angle lenses. Similarly, a business leader must also adjust their view to get the right picture. At times, they're going to need to look at the whole scene, and at times, a close-up is what they need to see. Both views are interconnected—and so is everything in between—as they are all part of the same subject. But depending on where and how you direct your focus, you'll get a completely different picture of what you're looking at.

Narrow and wide focuses mean zooming in and zooming out. It isn't that one type of focus is better than the other—we need both to function efficiently. Develop the competence to zoom in when you need to focus and to zoom out when you need to innovate, be creative, or get a wider perspective on things. With narrow focus, your brand name will have steady and stable growth. A narrow focus is the ability to attend to one or a limited number of goals at a time. It's the art of not spreading yourself too thin. In our experience, we've seen many companies that start out doing too many things, not understanding that sometimes this strategy is unattainable when you're just getting going as a small business.

What we need to understand first is how you narrow your focus. You may be selling too many products or services—known as taking on too much—which becomes unmanageable, especially for a small business. Large companies have the resources to manage this, but small businesses, and especially start-up companies, will need different advertising campaigns, websites, customer lists, inventories, vendors, salespeople, and accounting for each service or product line they offer. We see it all the time, for example, with construction companies that want to do large projects but end up pulled into smaller jobs. You can't keep up with it. You are pulling your hair out, losing sleep and your peace of mind. It's driving you crazy! We've often recommended to these types of clients that they narrow their focus, concentrating their efforts on doing fewer things but doing them very well. This approach can save time, money, and effort— and sometimes, even your business.

For the small business, think of your target customer base. It may be wiser to be selective rather than trying to capture the entire market. Target those who have a particular affinity to your product or service's unique attributes and customize your offer and message to attract them. When starting a new venture, offer only a few services that are solidly in your wheelhouse and that there is a market demand for, instead of taking the one-stop-shop approach, offering a multitude of services that you cannot support or manage. This strategy pays off in the long run, as you build a loyal customer base for your products and services. After you're more established and bringing in enough revenue, you can consider expanding your offerings and services to a wider customer base. At that point, you can increase the scope of your relationship with your customers, instead of lowering prices to attract new customers for existing products.

At first, narrowing your focus may seem like a bad idea from a mathematical standpoint. How can growth result from limiting opportunities? For our business, this strategy opened a world of opportunities not only in the United States but also Europe and Asia. The more engaged and focused we became with our early handful of clients, the more work they wanted to hire us for. We were able to cultivate a niche market, and this way we have been able to consistently grow our revenue. For a small business with few resources, less can actually be more, and, counterintuitively, can lead to increased profits.

Larger companies might be able to afford to do things differently, but no company got that way by going after twenty-nine million things at once. Even the largest companies, such as Amazon or Microsoft, focused on something narrow enough at first: books, or a computer operating system. In time, they greatly expanded their products and services. They went from a narrow focus to a wider one.

Narrow, focused efforts are important, but it is critical that an organization also continues looking wide and outward to keep watch for paths forward and storms of turbulence. With a wide focus, you're able to see a huge snapshot of your business—and see your larger vision for the future as well. This involves long-term planning and forward-thinking strategies that are not compartmentalized in just one or two categories. A business warrior takes care to develop a deep understanding of the finer points of their business through the narrow view but can also think of the larger whole, free to roam, dream, and ideate without preconceptions.

To thrive and grow, a business warrior needs a strong outward focus, especially to measure their impact on other people and organizations. This means you constantly compare the service or product you are providing with how it is consumed. When you have an inward focus, you tend to act to maximize your own advantages. But when you take on an outward focus, you seek a greater good beyond yourself. Outward focus brings a collective goal and collective effort to your organization. Having an outward focus is crucial for building strong relationships, fostering trust and collaboration, and achieving better outcomes for all involved.

Going wide also means pursuing different financial models of increasing revenue, diversifying your products and services, and preparing yourself for the future. According to McKinsey & Company, future-ready companies identify three characteristics: "who we are" as an organization, "how we operate," and "how we grow." They know who they are and what they stand for, and how they will grow by scaling up their ability to learn, innovate, and seek promising ideas regardless of their origin. By embracing these fundamentals, companies will improve their odds of thriving in the next normal.

But with a wide, outward focus come obvious challenges, like not being able to control every peripheral thing. A warrior in battle must complete an assignment and usually can't accomplish the largest objectives of the mission in that moment. Typically, their focus must be narrow. In business, you can waste resources if you're only operating wide, and a small business must be careful with its limited resources.

After determining the breadth of your focus, it's important to capture it and any other key objectives in writing. We've found that people are more successful when they write things down. Writing down what you intend to focus on—narrow, wide, outward—will allow you to identify the path you want to follow. It will offer you a clear direction, giving you the ability to adapt more quickly to changing environments, resulting in resiliency. It will also enable you to more easily dismiss the inevitable distractions that come up along the way. Write your focus down for your own clarity and to capture it for others, so you can share and communicate it to ensure alignment. In this way, writing down your focus also makes delegation easier.

Overcome the Temptation of Multitasking

When you're focused on your primary objective, you can still take in innovative ideas and explore new opportunities toward that end. You can listen well and be more successful at solving problems. But distractions always arise, so a business warrior needs to battle with these as they go all in. So much of our culture celebrates multitasking—it's a problem. We have too many things going on and too many tools that encourage us to juggle even more. A warrior must focus 100 percent on the moment.

Many businesses are so overloaded by multitasking, they're not focused on their approach to helping their clients. This has consequences. Warriors in business must have control of themselves, staying focused on the right things. So, rather than multitasking, pay attention to the people who are sharing their time and energy with you. Otherwise, you could miss something important or jeopardize the relationship. Set your phone or other personal agendas aside when you're with someone and focus your attention on them. Often, building solid relationships is much like driving. You have to keep your eyes on the road, knowing that anything could occur without warning. You can't text, or you might miss something happening on the road and lose the crucial seconds you need to act to save your own or someone else's life.

Sometimes multitasking can take the form of overextending and overloading yourself by forcing your business to be everything to everyone. This kind of multitasking can result in lack of clarity, which can kill your credibility. We've watched too many entrepreneurs try to do too many things at once. They don't end up doing any of them well and in the end get frustrated and quit. We believe this does a disservice to their clients and to themselves. Instead, focus on quality over quantity. You don't want to diminish the joy in your own entrepreneurial experience by overextending yourself early on.

MAKE THE MOST OF EACH DAY, KNOWING THE REST WILL TAKE CARE OF ITSELF.

The best way to avoid multitasking is to identify your priorities. Small-business leaders constantly need to prioritize. There are, at times, many fires burning at once. How do you know which to prioritize? A firefighter needs to look at these smaller fires as one wildfire—a complete scenario on its own—therefore assessing the situation and all its associated risks. While they can't put out fourteen fires at once, they *can* make their assessment of which they can address quickly and efficiently, avoiding the spread of new fires. Going all in means assessing the scene, understanding the level of importance, and managing the situation. In business, some fires automatically burn themselves out after a limited time, so if you develop your plan of attack carefully and wisely, you'll likely reach a more successful outcome.

A Sanskrit proverb says: "For yesterday is but a dream, and tomorrow is only a vision. But today, well-lived, makes every yesterday a dream of happiness and every tomorrow a vision of hope. So, look well therefore to this day." When a warrior in business is present in the moment, they can devote themselves fully to the actions that need to be taken now to achieve their greater goals in the future. Manage this day well, then do that again tomorrow and the day after that. Having the right focus and knowing what to take care of, and in what order, helps reduce the distracting temptation of multitasking. This is the way to make the most of each day, knowing the rest will take care of itself.

Put Negative Thoughts and Impulses in Their Place

Worries and concerns are normal and inevitable for any business owner. It's difficult to get a business off the ground, and you have a lot invested. When things don't go according to plan, it's easy to allow negative thoughts, anxieties, or fears to seep in, distracting you from what you need to do. You might be worried about cash flow, finding and retaining good employees, the downturn in the economy, cybersecurity, competitive forces, the state of the government, or cultural and social change, for instance. You might not know what will happen to your business in the next six months or even the next six weeks. But you cannot allow your worries and concerns to negatively influence decision-making. A warrior in business can't be incapacitated by negative thoughts. They can't afford to take their eyes off what's most important. Instead, they must find a way to overcome their worries or put them into proper perspective.

You need to be able to control your negative thoughts, so you know how to manage situations as they arise. Take a look at figure 2.1.

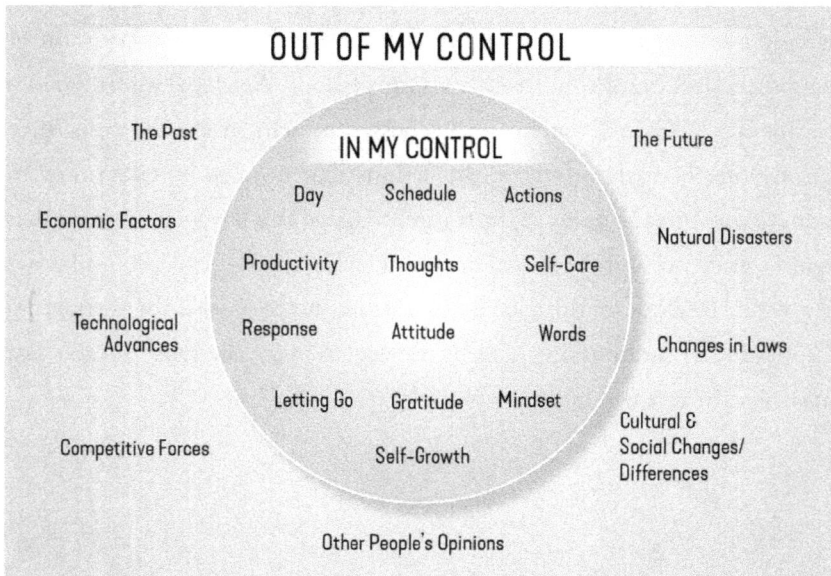

Figure 2.1

By having the right mindset about the circumstances of your business, you can learn how to let go of things that are out of your control and give yourself permission to do so. No one likes it when things are outside their control, but that's inevitable, so all you can do is give your absolute best. Accept that you must adapt as needed.

ACCEPT THAT YOU MUST ADAPT AS NEEDED.

Be attentive to what you can control. Some of these things will shape your decisions and responsibilities. Do not let the things that are outside your control overwhelm you and limit your ability to be effective with the things that are within your control. Declutter your mind from them and be at peace. Negativity hampers your potential. *You don't want to limit what you can achieve because you're stuck on things you can't control.* A warrior in business doesn't allow negative thoughts to distract them or hold them back.

Letting your worries go, of course, is easier said than done. But you can still make an informed decision about what to do. Do the research you need, collect data, and talk to experts. Use what you learn to make an informed decision about what to let go of and what to address. At the same time, know that letting certain things go is not an excuse for not taking action when needed.

The things that spark negative thinking can only negatively affect you if you allow them to. In fact, any adversity can be converted into a learning experience or opportunity. A warrior who goes all in looks at the big picture and takes each moment—good or bad—as it comes. By being intentional about getting the most out of each moment, you can transform adversity into something that betters your business.

In addition to worries, your feelings and impulses can sometimes dictate your choices. You need to know how to trust your gut without letting your negative feelings drive impulsive actions when you feel things are out of control. You can, in fact, exercise self-control when you're aware of what you're experiencing. Once you've regained your focus, you can make wise, data-driven decisions to improve your situation.

In our culture today, people tend to associate happiness with good and disappointment with bad. In real life, it's impossible to attain a state of constant happiness. You must recognize that you're going to be disappointed or unhappy about things at times, just as you'll be happy and content at other times. Resilience comes from knowing that the feelings come and go. When we understand that we'll fail at times but win at others, we can begin to approach our decisions with more resiliency. We don't have to act on impulse or react to a situation based on negative thoughts or feelings.

Recognize that your negative impulses are normal and natural. You can acknowledge them, but they don't have to become a distraction to your focus, ultimately driving you toward actions that don't serve your goals. Pay attention to what drives your impulses and feelings. Look at them honestly, but don't allow them to clutter your mind. Let go of these. Be open and flexible with what comes next. If your concerns about a situation are not aligned with your primary objectives, see if you can get past them or let them go. If you have a clear idea of what your focus is and can maintain it, you'll be able to align your efforts, energy, resources, finances, teams, and everything else with your goal.

Exercise: Conquering Distraction

Write down five distractions you face that prevent you from staying focused. Then, come up with five ways to enhance your ability to focus. Use this exercise to become aware of your habits or patterns, and intentionally attempt to improve your overall focus by addressing your distractions. We hope this provides you with greater clarity about where you are at the moment. Write them down for yourself and communicate them to others for accountability.

A business warrior knows themselves—when they do the up-front work, they are more effective when they go all in. This means ensuring they can stay focused in the moment and that they have the mental bandwidth to accomplish the mission free of unnecessary distractions. To do this, a warrior in business must clear their mind of unimportant things, which allows them to listen well and be more successful at solving problems in the moment. If they can accomplish this, they will be able to overcome adversity and be more resilient.

TAKE OWNERSHIP

When you go all in as a business warrior, you take ownership of all aspects of your organization: the operations, plans, and people. Ownership is about a lot more than just the financial stake you have in your company; it means your physical and emotional investment as well. You recognize that the responsibility is yours, and though you confer aspects of it to your team, it ultimately lies with you, and you accept it in full. It isn't just a percentage on a piece of paper—everyone at the company should be living it from the top down, no matter their role. It should be built into your company culture, and everyone should give 100 percent. When done right, everyone in your organization is living proof of your mission.

Ownership means you are willing to take risks, sacrifice, work hard, and accept your mistakes. In its truest sense, ownership is about taking initiative, believing that the actions needed to move the business forward are not someone else's responsibility; they're yours.

Taking ownership also means that you lead by example. Everything starts from the top—with you. When you take ownership of your business and make yourself accountable for doing what's needed, everyone knows they can trust you to do the right thing. In this way, you can foster a culture of trust and put systems and processes in place to carry your mission forward, and so you can trust your people to take ownership of their responsibilities.

Within a company, every team or project naturally has a leader, and everyone has something to contribute because they take ownership of their parts. You should have a system of checks and balances in place because that is also part of your responsibility when you take ownership. Checks and balances are very important. A warrior on a mission needs a map outlining the mission. If they're to march in a certain direction, that must be defined on the map or they won't get to where they are needed. You need the map to stay on the right path so your people know what's expected. Otherwise, you won't be able to accomplish what's needed. Your people will need you to share the standards you expect with them in advance. Later, you should have a way to compare the standards you set for them with their actual performance and the outcomes you see. These can take the form of regular one-to-one meetings, performance reviews, and ongoing conversations about growth and development. Your systems of checks and balances will help keep everyone grounded in reality so they can properly execute the mission.

Ownership is a word that can be used and abused. People say they take ownership and responsibility, but sometimes it's just lip service. True ownership and going all in is defined by action. It's something you can demonstrate and anyone can observe. Some leaders or team members like to take credit for successes but not failures. But when you take effective ownership, you own the outcome, whether it's a great success or a failure. Don't shy away from taking responsibility for the things that didn't work out. Learn and grow from them and use them to strengthen your team. When you demonstrate true, effective ownership, you will have a team that works well together and who can rely on you. If there's a problem, they will share responsibility, trust one another, and display unity, rather than engage in finger-pointing. No one will blame external factors or one another. Everyone will be engaged.

In your career, you've collaborated with people you could trust to get the job done, possibly even better than you expected. You've probably also worked with people who didn't deliver when they said they would, forgot to follow through, or just didn't get the job done. You felt like you couldn't trust them. This is because tied up in the concept of ownership is trust. As in life, when trust is broken in business, there are negative ramifications because we're all interconnected with our actions. A warrior can't go into battle if they can't trust their team. They must know that their team has their back, so they can perform at their utmost. A warrior in business goes all in by taking the ultimate responsibility and earning the trust of those around them. They understand that they are stronger and more effective when they put teams of responsible, trustworthy individuals in place to help move with them toward their objective.

A TEAM'S SUCCESS IS EVERYONE'S SUCCESS.

An essential tool for instilling a sense of ownership in a business from the top down is a concept called "belongingness." Belongingness is a collective feeling of unity shared across a company. When you help people cultivate the sense that they are part of your company and have a personal stake in it, they feel like it's their own, and they have a feeling of authority and shared ownership. They cease to be just employees, instead identifying as talented individuals who feel empowered and valued, knowing their ideas and efforts at the company matter. They're more willing to go above and beyond. This is part of building the culture of a company, a "we" culture. Real change and growth come from the support and involvement of a good team. Ownership allows a business warrior to build the kind of trustworthy, invested team that they need to overcome adversity, work sustainably, and be successful.

BE ACCOUNTABLE FOR ACCOMPLISHING THE MISSION

Accountability means you'll deliver as promised. It means you'll follow through. And, most challenging of all, it means holding yourself and your people responsible for their actions. It means acknowledging that the actions you take affect other team members' ability to accomplish their goals. Being accountable is a major factor in building trust, which empowers people to excel and exceed your expectations.

Being accountable is about being responsible for the results. As individuals, we hold ourselves accountable for the quality and timeliness of an outcome, even when we are working with others. When we, as business owners, and our people feel responsible, then we are building resilient teams that drive a resilient business, one that can weather the storms.

Accountability that builds trust, ownership, and follow-through is more relevant than ever before. Because of the global pandemic and advances in technology, team members are not working from one place, and sometimes not even from the same country. So, without good accountability in place, the effects on your businesses can be devastating. It's crucial in the workplace, but especially the remote workplace. When there is no system of accountability in place, things can fall apart very quickly.

How to Hold Yourself and Your Team Accountable

- Create a shared vision.
- Walk the talk. As an owner, you set the example for your company by being the role model of accountability for your people.
- Set realistic and measurable goals. They should be quantifiable. For example, if a report needs to be done, set a finish date and time.
- Engage and motivate your people.
- Create to-do lists.

In today's business climate, accountability will help you and your company to stay agile in response to business challenges.

GIVE YOUR ABSOLUTE BEST

A warrior in business knows that "good enough" is not enough to win the battle. Saying you're doing quality work is not enough. Quality should be the baseline you start from, but always aim to rise above it. Quality should simply be what's expected.

We often see company mission statements that declare they do quality work. But in a way, that means nothing. It's like saying you're going to do only as much as is needed. We should all be asking ourselves how we can go above and beyond, how we can give more to our clients. Are we going up from the baseline or operating below it? To be resilient in business, you must get noticed for doing stellar work in today's increasingly competitive global market. You should always vouch for the quality of your products and services, but simply saying you do quality work isn't enough.

Giving your absolute best means you're willing to work hard and sacrifice to get the job done. There's no success without sacrifice and hard work—it doesn't just come quickly and easily. Sometimes, it requires slow, steady, intentional progress that leads to longtime resilience.

Part of giving your absolute best involves setting goals. You set goals and develop the map we mention earlier in this chapter that lays out the course of action to reach those goals. Without those goals, you don't have a map people can follow. Certainly, your team can try to move toward the desired outcome, but a lot can go wrong or slow you down along the way. Methodology is part of the map. However you decide to get there, your methodology is what you're going to use to arrive at your destination. The methodology, or means of travel you use, determines the journey. Along the way, you must work with the mindset that with the absolute best effort you expend, there's nothing more you could possibly do to make it better. This doesn't mean sacrificing time with your loved ones or letting your health or other parts of your life suffer. Work and life balance is important for long-term resilience, and that includes setting your priorities in advance. Going all in and doing it in a way that reflects your absolute best means you are disciplined and intentional. It means you work smarter, not just harder. If you need to, take the input from your outcome and revise the way you have managed things, so you can improve the process and methodology the next time around. It's okay if you must figure things out as you go, discovering, for example, that you've spent too long in a particular area, but then just adjust, learn, and grow. Allow what you learn to become part of your methodology—and use that to drive your absolute best.

Break your goals down into smaller objectives: manageable, bite-size goals you can accomplish one day at a time. In our business, we've each made it a habit the night before to write down five to seven items we want to accomplish the next day. The discipline of this routine helps us to focus, visualize, and set the most important goals at the top of the list, knowing what we need to accomplish. These lists help keep us from becoming distracted and from multitasking in ways that are not productive. When you start your workday with a more productive and action-oriented mindset, it's easier for you to stay focused on the important goals, prevent distractions and challenges when they arise, and rearrange your priorities as time demands.

Plato said, "The first and greatest victory is to conquer self." Leading ourselves and others all comes down to discipline and commitment to giving your absolute best. That means making the right choices, having a clear vision, setting goals, maintaining high standards, and having a focus and framework on which to base important business decisions and actions. These are the elements around which you need to create your action plan.

SET YOUR TEAM IN MOTION

None of the planning and preparation you do will bring about your desired outcome without action. While it's true that a warrior in business needs to prepare and develop the right mindset beforehand, if they don't follow through with action, all their efforts will be wasted. To make it in business, execution is everything. As a small business owner or leader, you must make sure you're fully prepared—with your people and your systems—and then your execution can go smoothly.

Once you have created a culture of accountability, execution should occur smoothly, uninterrupted, and without drama because you have instilled a feeling of ownership and collaboration among your team members, and they have a vested interest in not letting you down. When it's time to execute, just watch and trust your people. They will deliver. If you have the right systems in place and the kind of culture that upholds them, the action in a company can take care of itself in many instances. You can step back and do the strategic work a leader needs to do, knowing your team continues to execute on the programs, events, or projects you put in place. They'll be able to manage what's needed because

- You've communicated what the plan is
- They understand the expectations
- They understand the steps and why they've been laid out in a particular way
- They know what their roles are and what teams they'll serve on

In other words, everyone is on the same page and understands the task at hand. They know where the starting line is, what the steps are, what the expected timeline is, and what the finish line looks like. Between the starting line and the finish line is where all the key components come into play: setting the focus, preparation, and planning; outlining the process;

defining the methodology; determining the responsibilities; establishing the trust; inviting collaboration; and ensuring ownership and accountability. This is the framework you must set as a business owner to ensure effectiveness when your team executes.

SET ACHIEVABLE GOALS AND SET YOURSELF AND YOUR TEAMS UP FOR SUCCESS.

Of course, success is not guaranteed when you go all in, but you do need to commit fully to your goals to achieve them. This commitment comes from a focus on defining those goals and establishing top priorities. Start with a few things at a time, and then take on more as you proceed.

The term "warrior" conjures up images of battles and fighting, but a warrior is also tactically trained. It's not *all* about warfare; it's also about keeping peace, upholding principles, bringing out the best in people, and leading the group toward a shared common goal. When a warrior goes all in, they're engaged in such a way that yields benefits for those they serve. This is the real purpose and meaning behind the work you do.

Executive Summary

- To succeed in business, you must "go all in" and be **fully committed and personally invested.**

- Knowing **what your priorities are** will help you determine how to invest your energy and attention.

- Realize that in any given situation, **you cannot do anything more than your best**.

- **Success is a journey**, not a particular result or outcome.

- **Be present, in the present.**

- Be aware of both your **narrow and wide focuses** in business. Narrowing your focus can help you maximize your strengths and minimize weaknesses, and widening your focus can help you strategize long-term growth.

- **Do not engage in multitasking.** You must be present in the current moment to achieve your goals in the day-to-day, as well as long term.

- Do not let the **things that are outside your control** overwhelm you and limit your ability to be effective with the things that are within your control.

- **Taking ownership of your responsibilities** will earn the trust of your team and drive your business forward.

- **Taking accountability is about being responsible for the results.** It can help your company stay agile in response to business challenges.

- **Set high standards for the quality of your work** so you make a habit of doing your absolute best.

- Make sure you are **fully prepared with the right people and systems**, and your business will run smoothly.

CHAPTER 3

A WARRIOR IN BUSINESS IS DECISIVE

DECISIVENESS IS CRITICAL FOR A WARRIOR IN business. In a battle, warriors don't always have enough time to think through all the factors; situations can call for an immediate response. Oftentimes, if you hesitate, you can miss out on an opportunity. Your inactivity can cost you. Unless you know how to make smart, strategic decisions in the moment, you cannot act. A warrior in business understands that the work of decision-making can be cultivated before the moment in which it is required. That way, you can achieve more clarity about an unexpected situation and more confidently decide on a good course of action at the time you need to.

With experience comes the realization that the process around *making* a decision is often more important than the decision itself. There are great benefits to focusing on the process rather than the eventual outcome. This strategy allows you to remain clearheaded in any given moment, weigh the relevant information, make timely decisions, and act. It also grants you flexibility in any situation, so you can make quick adjustments as events unfold.

BE MENTALLY PRESENT

To know how to make good, smart decisions in the heat of battle, a warrior needs to be mentally present. This means staying focused and keeping their mind free of distractions. Without all the white noise, they're more aware, alert, and attentive. In a battle, they need to keep their senses sharp, carefully observing every nuance of what's happening around them. Missing something crucial could literally cost them their lives.

In the business-is-war world we live in today, the stakes are high. To thrive and not just survive, you need to be 100 percent present, even in the smaller, everyday operational aspects of your organization. Taking just twenty to thirty seconds to quickly respond to a text in the middle of a meeting could cause you to miss a crucial part of the conversation. Suppose you had to jump in and act, based on what was discussed? Would you have the facts you needed? In a world inundated with smartphones, social media, quick web searches, chats, and emails, you may find yourself distracted in the workplace now more than ever. When you're distracted, you can fail to make the right decision at the right time. It could cost you missed opportunities, whether they be financial, informational, or relational.

Not being all there in the moment also decreases your overall productivity. Over time, this can lead to huge losses for a small company. When you're not attentive and committed to the things you've taken on, you lose the ability to act effectively. In these moments, you're not armed with the information you need to think clearly and quickly about what to do. Being mentally, physically, and emotionally present puts you in a better position to get ahead and act in demanding situations, problem-solve, create, innovate, and transform situations for the better. Developing this kind of mind training is a soft skill, but, when practiced, it allows you to achieve a whole lot. At the same time, when you have this kind of mental acuity, you can bring out other strengths and let them shine—charisma, composure, better communication, and the ability to notice details about other people or projects.

Lots of companies recognize that mindfulness, which drives decision-making, is more than a technical skill. It's essential for the health and growth of their talent pipelines. It's no secret that corporate giants like Google, General Mills, Intel, Aetna, Goldman Sachs, and Fidelity Investments offer mindfulness training to employees.[3] According to *Harvard Business Review*, mindfulness research shows that investing in reflection, openness, and thoughtfulness will have a positive impact on employees and on the bottom line. It results in higher-quality interactions, informed decisions, emotional intelligence, and it boosts resilience to stress and improves mental focus.

Mind training leads to flexible, adaptable, creative, and courageous thinking. Mind training is a crucial part of decision-making because it keeps distractions and agitation away and allows you to stay calm, clear, and focused. Given where your business is and what your challenges are, consider what this practice might look like for you.

To develop in this area, start by putting yourself in a calm state of mind. Be clear and focused. Practice this every day and in different situations, recognizing that it's an ongoing, evolving process, a habit that requires some rituals. For us, part of our ritual is to look at our to-do list every morning before the day begins. This keeps us calm, focused, clear-minded,

---

3   Kimberly Schaufenbuel, "Why Google, Target, and General Mills Are Investing in Mindfulness," *Harvard Business Review*, December 28, 2015, https://hbr. org/2015/12/why-google-target-and-general-mills-are-investing-in-mindfulness.

and in a state of readiness. We know what's before us, and if anything else crops up, we at least know the parts of ourselves that we can control. A ritual is having a cup of coffee in the morning while you look over emails. It can be that simple. If you work remotely, your ritual may entail dressing for work before you enter your home office, so you put yourself in the mindset that you're now in work mode.

To figure out what rituals would best serve you, first set short-term and long-term goals that are achievable. Make sure you are clear on why the goals you set are important and then focus on developing your skills, not just on the achievement or outcomes. Stay flexible if the situation changes, tweak your goals, monitor your progress, and adjust as needed. We recommend preparing a schedule. Set boundaries for your time. If waking up and going to bed early makes sense for your life, do that. The right lifestyle changes can relieve tension and anxiety and allow you to become more mentally present. Ensure that there are clear separations between your personal and professional life. Create and dedicate time for yourself. Take time to exercise, walk in nature, read a book, listen to music, meditate, meet a friend, cook, or help a charity or cause. Do whatever brings clarity and joy to your mind.

Clearheadedness leads to the ability to be mentally present. When you are present, you're not wishy-washy, and it doesn't then take forever for you to make up your mind. When you are purposeful, committed, and resilient, you can be decisive. You can more confidently stick to your decisions and have conviction behind them.

BE DECISIVE OR RISK FAILURE

Timing is a critical part of the decision-making process. Often, you may hesitate to make decisions out of fear of making the wrong choices. You may experience nervousness or discomfort that bars you from making the decisions necessary to achieve success. This usually stems from a fear of failure, and this incapacitates you in many ways. But a warrior can't just freeze on the battlefield; they risk failure from inaction. In the same way, indecisiveness in your organization can stop or slow things down. Don't be afraid to be decisive—that fear makes you lose your ability to think flexibly. It limits you, causing you to stick only to what you know, what is comfortable and familiar. It prevents you from making a decision, moving forward, and, ultimately, succeeding.

FEAR OF FAILURE CAN LEAD YOU STRAIGHT TO FAILURE ITSELF.

You need to be a warrior rather than a worrier. It's okay to make a mistake. You should approach your mistakes not as failures but as opportunities to learn and gain experience. You don't have to repeat mistakes—that much is within your control. You may not always know exactly the right thing to do in the moment, but when you make the decision, stand behind it and be committed to it. Once you've seen the outcome, you can make the modifications you need, consider the next steps, and address what's needed so things can go better the next time. Ditch your fear to allow yourself the freedom to pursue the options available to you.

Don't let the different internal conflicts that play out in your mind lead to procrastination or inaction. A warrior faces actual combat; they can't afford to engage in mini wars in their own mind, getting stuck on worst-case scenarios. Allowing yourself to let this go will give you a better outcome and allow you to move forward.

In Hinduism, Lord Krishna, the god of compassion, protection, and love, is traditionally thought of as a great warrior and philosopher. He offers teachings for better decision-making, telling us to be present and to be clear-minded, focused, and convicted. The epic poem, the *Bhagavad Gita*, tells of a warrior named Arjuna who feels a deep internal conflict about following his duty to fight as a warrior. He discusses this discord in his mind with Lord Krishna, who tells Arjuna that he must use his wisdom to choose how best to proceed. Lord Krishna recognizes that internal conflict has caused Arjuna to freeze, and that the only counsel the warrior really requires is that he must make a decision at that moment, instead of staying stuck in his thoughts.

Because of our social training and upbringing, we all tend to be results-based. You may find that you focus a lot of your thinking on the results or outcomes and often create different scenarios in your mind around your fears or negative outcomes. This causes you to freeze, procrastinate, and not choose a course of action. But the worst fears you experience might only be happening in your own mind. According to chapter 2, verse 47 of the *Bhagavad Gita*, "You have the right to perform your prescribed duty, but don't cultivate a sense of entitlement for the fruits of your action." In other words, the results are going to happen in the future, which can be affected by many external factors we have no control over. Do your duty and do your best now. Control what you can, move forward, stand behind your decision, and the outcome will arrive. It may not be nearly as bad as you feared, and in some cases, it could be better than you expected.

Having established all this, we do want to make the distinction between unproductive fear and healthy fear. Healthy fear is not a bad thing: It can allow us to be cautious and aware. But a warrior, when training their mind, must learn how to see the difference between the two. And they need to look at the big picture. In the case of Arjuna, he wrestled with whether to fulfill his duty and responsibility to fight. His responsibility wasn't just to engage in war but also to fight for the greater good. As a business leader, you must recognize that your duties are to your customers, clients, shareholders, partners, and employees. You can't relinquish your responsibilities or duties.

Mental and emotional strengths are skills we can learn and develop. When you have trained your mind to stay focused on the process and not on the outcome, you will be freer to move forward in making decisions—even the ones that seem the hardest to make. You will face challenges, changes, and pressures. But if you maintain the right mindset during your decision-making, you can face adversity, recover from setbacks, and ultimately come out better, thus fighting for the greater good of your organization and people.

LEAVING YOUR COMFORT ZONE IS THE ONLY WAY TO DRIVE ACTION.

Some people procrastinate because they like to remain in their comfort zones. The warrior in action must get out of their comfort zone to make any progress. And so do you. This involves a willingness to change and experience something that might feel a little scary or out of your control, which isn't easy. For a turtle to move forward, it needs to come out of its shell and stick its neck out. It may feel like a bit of a risk to do so, but the turtle will be confined to one place unless it moves from its comfort zone.

Periodically, you'll want to review and think about what additional progress you want to make. Where are you too comfortable and unconsciously barring yourself from making a good decision and moving forward?

While acting expediently is key, you must also try not to make hasty decisions before you have the information you need, as these can have negative effects on your desired outcome. Many times, a warrior needs to think and pause to weigh the right course of action and evaluate and analyze the facts. You might feel compelled to decide on something for the sake of deciding. But in certain instances, the best decision is not to decide but rather to put something on the shelf and let time sort it out. In those cases, the decision to do nothing *is* the decision itself. It is a choice grounded in information, not driven by fear, and it's a choice that's focused on your goal. This choice can allow you to avoid making a decision that you have to backpedal on. If you have the time to let it work itself out, sometimes that's the wisest thing to do.

ARM YOURSELF WITH INFORMATION

A warrior arrives at a good decision based on knowledge, experience, and expertise. A warrior in business chooses to invest time and effort in their own development through education, training, and learning new skills. Otherwise, they are at a disadvantage that won't allow them to think at their highest level and thoughtfully respond in the moment.

So, where do you seek out the information you need? One great resource is to talk with trusted advisors, professionals, or other business owners. They can be from within your industry, but great advice also comes from those outside of your field. Or you may seek out the thoughts of your clients, suppliers, and business partners. It is a myth that asking for help demonstrates weakness. It's tough to be resilient in business all alone. Even a warrior needs to rely on help and information from other soldiers from time to time. They're fighting the same fight. Often, you may find yourself trying to do everything you can alone before asking for someone's assistance or insight, but good leaders recognize that their strength lies in their people and partnerships. They have things to learn, and they have information to share. They understand that they can benefit from the help of others in certain areas and can offer assistance to others in their areas of strength.

It's critical to know when to ask for help and who you should approach for it. You may have a professional mentor or coach or know another expert who can offer a fresh perspective and objective thinking around a decision you need to make. Maybe you're part of a professional organization or have a circle of trusted friends. Getting the opinions of those you trust can provide you with the insights you need. It can also validate your decisions, giving you extra confidence in your decision-making abilities.

Also, people aren't your only source of help. Study market trends or trends in the global economy. Read up on industry news. Take professional development courses. Attend conferences and workshops. Look at research that's relevant to what you do. The idea is to stay informed about what is happening in your space. As you do this, take care to ensure your sources are credible and current. Nowadays, we need to be aware of misinformation. Don't seek validation from those who are seeking it for themselves. Know when to explore alternate options.

Collect what you need, then weigh the information to determine what's factual, what's useful, and what's applicable. If we don't get all the information we need, it could be that we're operating without certain necessary facts or perspectives. This could lead to a flawed decision-making process. You don't have to take everything at face value, but you also don't want to miss something beneficial.

HOW TO TAKE ACTION: PROCESS MAPPING

Being decisive means choosing the right things that can expand your opportunities. A warrior in business understands how to make a plan to maximize these opportunities. To be resilient in today's business climate, you need to be the quickest and brightest thinker, a mission-driven innovator, and a leader able to identify pain points, inefficiencies, and breakdowns in the decision-making process.

We talked earlier about belongingness and accountability. When these elements are part of your company culture, your decision-making will become easier, and you'll receive fewer rejections from people about the decisions you make. People will feel as if they're part of the decision. And because everyone in your organization will be engaged in the process of decision-making, you will have more buy-in, more investment, and happier employees who feel like their voices and opinions are considered. They can feel like they're equally contributing toward the one shared goal you all have.

Process mapping is a visual that uses charts, flowcharts, and symbols to answer the following three essential questions:

1. What are the tasks in the process?

2. Who performs each task?

3. When does each task occur?

Process mapping is a graphic representation of major and minor steps to take to achieve your action plan, and it can improve your decision-making. You can use it to assist all members, helping them see and understand the details, determining how every stakeholder is involved. Through it, you can gain a better understanding of a technical or business process. You map out a plan people can see and follow.

Process mapping is used in many facets of our business and personal lives. We do it every day when we mentally decide to take a step in any scenario. In the business world, this process is more formalized to document each action that needs to be taken. It is amazing that when you put your thought process on paper, it becomes clearer, and you may start to see what people or steps need to be added or removed from your plan.

Depending on what's required, you can do this at the macro, thirty-thousand-foot level, allowing you to see the project or whole decision in a larger way, or take a micro, five-thousand-foot view, narrowing things down to a more focused area of your decision-making process. What you choose will be based on your input and output. Your input could involve mentors who guide you in your decision process, or it could mean relying on the knowledge and wisdom you gain through extensive reading; participating in conferences; taking online courses; or examining blogs, podcasts, and other resources. As you analyze and improve the input in your decision-making process, you'll find yourself believing more in the decisions you make, sticking to your plans, and leading more effectively. Analyzing output is an invaluable practice because it can help individuals and organizations understand the results of their efforts by recognizing improvement areas, making informed decisions about allocating resources, and optimizing processes to increase impact.

THERE IS NO PERFECT PROCESS.

For even greater clarity, you can combine a micro and macro focus with other tools, like the SWOT analysis, measuring strengths, weaknesses, opportunities, and threats on your process map. Note that creating a process map also calls for you to review expectations because when you make a decision, you're also looking for some expectation. Using a specific tool for the wrong purpose may not be fruitful. Know that process maps, as insightful as they can be, have their own limitations. Trying to create a perfect process map is impossible. There is no perfect process.

EXPECT TO PIVOT AND ADJUST

Mahatma Gandhi once said, "Adaptability is not imitation. It means power of resistance and assimilation." Companies that are willing to pivot and adapt to changing market situations and conditions are more likely to succeed in the long run.

One example of a company that successfully pivoted is PayPal. Initially, PayPal was a company that developed security software for handheld devices. However, the company soon realized its product needed to gain traction in the market. PayPal pivoted to become an online payment system, which turned out to be a highly successful move. Another example is Twitter, which started as a platform for podcasting. It didn't perform as its founders had expected, so they planned the most crucial step in Twitter's history—a hackathon at which Jack Dorsey announced a new idea for an incredibly simple product.

The nature of any business is dynamic. You must know when to adjust and adapt to new situations, modify your plan, or be willing to go in a new direction. Don't be afraid to *not* follow the norm. Sometimes, you may need to change the business model, stand up to create something worthwhile, or come up with an innovation capable of changing the entire course of your business. It could be the very decision you need to make.

Take the example of Southwest Airlines. Decades ago, this airline let go of the traditional path and chose something different to better serve customers. It created a new market niche for travelers who wanted a cheap, easy, and convenient experience. Southwest did not follow the norm of commercial aviation at the time but rather came up with smaller planes and one type of aircraft. It no longer offered first class or in-flight meals, and it pared down its food offerings to simple snacks. The experience was simplified, and the company has remained profitable all these years without furloughs and layoffs.

Similarly, FedEx took a different approach to shipping. In earlier days, deliveries were from point A to point B, but FedEx chose to implement the hub concept, in which all deliverables go to specific hubs for sorting before being moved to smaller transports for delivery to the nearest designated point. Today, the hub model has been adopted by all couriers involved in delivery services.

Pivoting, adjusting, and innovating can happen either when a business is just starting out and its leadership chooses to break the mold from the start, or when an existing business is thriving and is in a good enough position to try something outside the norm. But sometimes the opposite is true: Businesses that are failing may need to do something completely different to survive.

This kind of pivoting was abundant in the restaurant industry in the weeks and months immediately following the first COVID lockdown, when restaurants had to change the way they served their customers. Some restaurants eliminated buffets, while others increased spacing between tables. As the lockdowns continued, many pivoted to providing new outdoor seating options and offering curbside pickup and delivery services. With rising costs at the time and fewer workers, restaurants had to focus on doing what they could to retain customers and revenue. They improved customer service, brought in new technology, and found ways to keep their businesses profitable.

When you're considering bigger changes like this, it's important to step back, evaluate, analyze, and think carefully about how such modifications can even be implemented. What's the vision? What problems does it solve? Then, you have to spend time preparing. Gather the information you need, talk to other business owners, and build your resources. For a small company, pivoting this way can entirely change the fate of your business.

Recognize also that the decisions you make today will not necessarily affect tomorrow. You may need to expend energy and other resources to sow seeds that don't offer you a lot of advantages today but will provide for your company in the future. You still need to plant the seeds, fertilize, and water them. One day, the results will appear. Overall, 90 percent of the work you do now will probably be for today, but it's important to ensure that 10 percent of what you do will help take care of you tomorrow.

Any business decision you make needs to be for the greater purpose and resiliency of your organization. Your decisions must have conviction, must bring equality, must be high standard, must be ethical, and cannot be based on selfishness, greed, anger, or resentment.

Just as a warrior on the battlefield must be prepared to adjust strategy to account for changes in weather, troop readiness, or enemy movements, a business warrior must do what's needed to adapt to changes in their market, industry, or global community. Without this agility, your business cannot move forward. Along with this agility, a decisive mindset in the face of uncertainty is crucial in making smart, strategic decisions in the moment to ensure the future of your business. By focusing on clarity of purpose, by considering the counsel of peers and mentors you trust, and by being willing to leave your comfort zone without fear of failure, you can bring wisdom and confidence to your decision-making process, which may mean the difference between success and failure for you, your team, and your company.

Executive Summary

- For your company to thrive, you need to be **100 percent present**, even in the smaller, everyday operational aspects of your organization.

- **Mindfulness drives decision-making** and keeps distractions away, allowing you to stay calm, clear, and focused.

- **Don't be afraid to be decisive**—feeling fear makes you lose your ability to think flexibly.

- The only way to make the decisions that will drive action is to **leave your comfort zone**.

- Good leaders don't try to do everything alone and **recognize that their strength lies in their people** and partnerships.

- You must be able to **identify inefficiencies and breakdowns** in your decision-making process.

- Business is dynamic, so **don't be afraid to innovate or modify your previous plans** to remain competitive in a changing market.

- Don't forget to **plan for the future**. While 90 percent of the work you do now may be for today, it's important to ensure that 10 percent of what you do will help provide for your company tomorrow.

CHAPTER 4

A WARRIOR IN BUSINESS FACES THE AMBUSH

IN A BATTLE OR WAR, AN AMBUSH is a surprise attack, but ambushes happen in a business context too. In fact, they happen almost every day. They're a certainty and a reality for all business owners. Unforeseen opponents always stand ready to attack you in unknown and unpredictable ways, and even if you devise strategies to avoid being ambushed, you can't always predict when an ambush is going to happen or prepare adequately for every situation. That's the nature of surprises.

In the same way battleground ambushes seem to materialize out of nowhere, in a business environment, unforeseen circumstances can happen at any time. For example, you might suddenly lose a major client, be met with opposition from your teams around a certain initiative, find that a new competitor has emerged, experience a breakdown of a key piece of equipment, or get trapped into a false agreement. On top of that, we face additional threats in the world that are beyond our control but affect our organizations. The challenges are endless: COVID, disrupted supply chains, natural disasters caused by climate change, financial or economic crises that affect global markets, new technologies, or even new regulations that make the old way of doing things no longer feasible.

By nature, small businesses are heavily invested, and their leadership often stands at the front lines of these kinds of attacks. So, how can you avoid being left wide open or thrown off track? How can you navigate through the unexpected challenges that will arise? This is where your true test of leadership lies. Are you going to be a resilient leader who can bring about a good resolution in any situation?

Unexpected challenges present an opportunity for a warrior in business to show resiliency. You can use these real-time tests to demonstrate your courage, ingenuity, and strength. Your ability to manage your business for the long haul is determined by how you lead through distress, challenges, and turbulence today. When you're confronted with these complicated and alarming scenarios, it can be scary, nerve-racking, and difficult to know what to do. But these can also be your finest hours. Don't let the unexpected hold you back or throw you off. In these times, a warrior uses their strategic knowledge, tactical training, and experience in battle to think ahead, formulate a plan of attack, and minimize injury to those who will be affected.

STEP INTO THE UNKNOWN

Unknowns are uncomfortable in our personal lives and business. How can a warrior possibly plan for every scenario? You can't. But you *can* conceptualize unknowns as experiences and knowledge you are yet to gain.

Some small-business leaders are averse to stepping into the unknown. But when faced with an impending situation, moving courageously into the unknown is an action—it is a proactive approach to meeting the problem head-on.

To succeed, business owners and leaders need to be willing to face the unknown. From the standpoint of personal development, it's important for the revitalization of your mind. You must look to the positive side of the unknown. Unknown challenges can move you forward, bringing you new knowledge, experiences, and revelations that may sharpen your skills as a leader. Ambushes can shed light on a path to growth, and you can evolve and elevate the work you do when you embrace them. Ambushes may also point to areas you have not paid much attention to.

You need to leave your comfort zone to be an effective leader. Lean into your mind; draw from what you've learned; and use your innate talent, passions, resources, and networks to tackle unexpected situations. You must be willing to explore a new area and take a leap of faith. In so doing, you might not just reveal who you are but also *define* who you are, what your purpose is, and why you do what you do in business. Rather than shying away from the unknown, accept it, prepare for it, and seek out the good in it.

Unknown situations may call for thoughtful actions but not for overthinking. Overthinking may result in anxiety and stress, and if this cycle of worry, anxiety, or panic persists, it will not only prevent you from acting but also result in disappointments and setbacks. It can make you feel incapacitated and prevent you from reaching your goals. Don't let overthinking overshadow your mind or slow you down.

A warrior develops a fearless state of mind that is open and invites positive change. This state of mind empowers you to start with fresh, innovative ideas. You're able to shake out of the old environment, which may not have been healthy for your growth mindset. You don't have to be afraid of rejection or failure. Jumping in and embracing the challenge is the answer. A warrior understands what they have to offer—their personal value and contribution. Rather than shrinking away from a challenge, they throw off the fear of rejection and take action to see if they can bring success out of it. They keep trying, learning, and improving as they go.

Many renowned figures have dealt with rejection and hardship multiple times before building a new life and career. Milton Hershey's first two candy companies failed, but he kept trying and eventually founded the world-renowned Hershey chocolate company. Thomas Edison's inventions failed more often than they succeeded, but he is considered one of the greatest inventors of all time. Oprah Winfrey, born into poverty, faced great hardship and tragedy in her youth, but she didn't let it hold her back and she became one of the most influential talk-show hosts and television producers of our time. And Theodor Geisel, whose first book was rejected by twenty-seven publishers before finally being accepted, became a much-loved and widely read children's book author, writing under the pen name Dr. Seuss.

LEARN, ADJUST, BE FLEXIBLE, AND ADAPT.

When we're met with opposition or seemingly insurmountable obstacles, we don't have to get stuck there. We can pick up the pieces, stand up taller, rebuild what needs to be rebuilt, and start over again from there. No failure, rejection, or challenge is a loss if you use it as fuel and inspiration for moving forward.

Buddha had to escape from his royal family before he changed his life and discovered his path to enlightenment. He had no clue what would happen when he left the safety of the only life he had ever known. All he knew was that there was a higher calling for him, and it required him to get out of his comfort zone.

When you start a new business, you're faced with all sorts of unknowns. You may not know exactly how things will turn out: how much revenue you're really going to generate, how your clients will receive you, or how your suppliers will support you. But it's important to face these uncertainties and do what you can. By mapping out your business, whether you do it in your mind or on a piece of paper, you can help guide the outcome. You can begin giving shape to the unknown and doing tangible things to make positive actions become reality.

THINK ON YOUR FEET

Even with prior knowledge and training, you cannot really plan or prepare for an ambush. An ambush can happen in the blink of an eye, and in that moment, you'll have to act immediately. Maybe you need to run toward the situation; or take a quick step to the side, turn, and rally the troops around you; or launch a new counteroffensive. In a battle situation, you're in the line of fire, faced with new factors and circumstances, uncertain about the outcome, and you need to be able to think on your feet to figure out the next action you take.

In business, when you're in the hot seat, you need to be able to improvise quickly and wisely. It matters how clearly you think under pressure, what you say and do next, and how you react. People might be watching, you might have a lot of money on the line, and your reputation might be at stake.

The Five C's of Improvisation

Improvisation is a function of uncertainty, unpredictability, and unexpected developments. How do we gain agility in the face of ambiguity and time pressure? Improv is a state in which a business warrior accepts what is presented, without judgment, and offers up something in return. And if we remember that this is not about perfection, and it's not all on you to have all the answers, then that can be a game changer.

In these times, as you think on your feet, we recommend you engage the Five C's.

1. **Confidence**—There is a phrase in improv: "Bring a brick, not a cathedral." Confidence can come from simply making an effort, no matter how small that may be.

2. **Courage**—War is won or lost in your head, not your hands. The more we dare to confront our fears, the more our brains are wired for courage. We become creative. We step out of our comfort zone. Courage is not getting up on stage and failing but getting up on stage again after you've failed.

3. **Credibility**—Someone who has integrity in dealing with others and their obligations is responsible, trustworthy, and honest. You come through.

4. **Control**—The best way to improv is to let go of control and share the control. This also means accepting other people's ideas. You become a leader in charge and not a leader in control.

5. **Comfort**—Pushing beyond your comfort zones, you are thinking outside the box and come up with unique solutions that can give your business a competitive advantage.

Thinking on your feet is an important leadership quality. It is your ability to become comfortable with surprises, and it is a skill that you can improve. To do this, as with other things, you need to be fully present and focused. The earlier work you did of self-development, knowledge building, and training can better equip you to respond well during an encounter. In many turbulent situations, it's not about the speed but the accuracy of your action that gets you through.

To think on your feet and confidently respond to every situation takes bravery. It is about developing the mental agility to spin any surprise to your benefit and to comm_nicate with confidence and courage. How admirable it is to watch a skilled quarterback. They see what is in front of them and quickly make the changes needed to best deal with a situation in the middle of a play to gain the best possible outcome.

The same can be true in business. You can learn to do so many things instantly and intuitively that it becomes second nature. After a while, you can rely more on your gut feelings, experiences, knowledge, and instincts. Using these, you might be able to suddenly pull it all together to make it work. Some people are better at spontaneous action than others because they practice, practice, practice and seek out a good coach to help them improve. If you haven't yet developed in this way, you can still improvise and adapt to tricky situations, as well as look for ways to quickly recover from the obstacles that have gotten in your way.

Get Ready to Improvise

Improvisation is the ability to create and implement a new or an impromptu solution in the face of an unexpected problem or change. It is often seen as an impulsive, spontaneous, creative problem-solving personal behavior. *When you're ambushed, you are forced to improvise.* We believe the ability to improvise is key to being a successful warrior in business and to organizational agility and resilience.

In the business world, we often face situations where our execution within the moment determines success, much like it does on the stage. Business improvisation is the ability to understand a situation, to access your absolute best and apply it to the circumstance. It's thinking quickly, being confident and flexible enough to adapt your performance in real time to whatever gets thrown at you.

Improvisation is essential for human beings coming together in groups and making something out of nothing. It creates collaboration in teams who can objectively listen to one another, respect and support each other's ideas, and build on those ideas, which leads to better decision-making, enhanced problem-solving, and more creative working relationships.

You can't plan for every situation, but you can learn to become a capable and confident improviser who steers their company through these crises. One can never quite know what is waiting around the corner, no matter how much you try to prepare. Improvising well requires both intentional action and meaningful responses. To develop in this area, start by asking the right questions during challenging situations, engaging and collaborating with people to bring solutions to the larger problem. Look for fresh approaches and increase your ability to be creative.

YOU MUST IMPROVISE WITH JOY AND NOT HAVE THE SLIGHTEST FEAR OF LOSING.

To improvise effectively, you must watch and listen attentively, learn to respond with "yes, and" to the unexpected, and be willing to contribute. Daily practice will help you remain in the right state to cope and come across as credible, rather than panic-stricken. Fearlessly face failure. Be prepared to confront the unexpected. Remember that as a child you played freely without having to worry about who was watching and judging you. You need to improvise in the same way—with joy—and not have the slightest fear of losing. Creativity is a muscle that every human has, and to keep it strong you must stretch it regularly. *Improvising is about preparation and collaboration more than anything else.*

Many people think improvising means you're winging it—making things up as you go along. But in business, winging it isn't great, because it's not based on knowledge. In this case you may not only lose clients but also your credibility. No one wants to work long-term with a professional who continually flies by the seat of the pants, whether it's a salesperson, a doctor, an attorney, a teacher, or anyone else. Improvisation is different because there are long hours of preparation, practice, and sacrifices that go along with it. For any business leader, preparation is like a warm-up exercise that helps you build strong muscles, maintain stability, and be physically at your best.

Improvising in Business

Active Listening

The most important skill needed for improvising is listening. Listening skills are vital to a business-partnering approach. Only by listening can you understand the other person's goals and objectives and their pain points, and from there help them make decisions and warn them of any consequences.

In a business context, the art of listening helps persuade, influence, and build rapport. In this unpredictable business landscape, organizations that have equipped their people with the ability to improvise are those that will cope more effectively when crisis situations arise.

Nonverbal Cues

Posture, facial expressions, and eye contact can speak volumes. If you understand what the other person is thinking and what is going through their mind by observing their nonverbal cues, you can more effectively collaborate.

Effective Communication

From impromptu conversations to speaking in public to answering an unexpected question after a presentation, your preparation, education, and experience, along with clarity and conciseness, will make you more effective at improvising.

To face an ambush, you need to be able to improvise, not wing it. Prepare as much as you practically can for the unknown. Be a winner, not a winger.

RESPOND APPROPRIATELY

Whether you are facing an unexpected, angry accusation in a business meeting or a challenge triggered by something totally unknown to you, how you respond to the situation can make the difference between exacerbating the problem and diffusing it. Your ability to transcend the situation and turn it into something good is dependent on your own competence.

Summon Your Best Response in an Ambush

1. **Prepare yourself**—As much as possible, prepare for potential ambushes in advance. When you plan things out, you build a framework for success. If you fail to do so, you're already starting out at a deficit. Build strong and defensive boundaries that can empower you to be resilient when a challenge arises. You not only save yourself but also arm your responses with more courage and confidence. In business, having healthy boundaries means clarifying responsibilities and expectations. It means taking accountability for your own actions and results and working in a way that helps others to solve their own problems—instead of taking responsibility for them yourself. A good team member will take responsibility for their team's work and results—especially if the results are unexpected and they're in a position of leadership. People with weak or no boundaries are often exhausted and irritable, feel guilty and anxious, and have trouble making decisions. This can lead to chaotic teams and unmanageable work environments. Having strong defensive boundaries leads to confidence, emotional stability, and reduced anxiety—giving you a sense of control.

2. **Maintain situational awareness**—The best way to survive an ambush is to avoid being caught in one in the first place. Know what's happening around you. Be alert and informed. Listen and observe. For small businesses, it is important to have a business plan, an ever-evolving document that you can regularly reassess and amend to reflect the current happenings within your field. The more you stay up to date with

your clients' needs and expectations and the business tools you need to operate efficiently, the better your chances of preventing traps of self-sabotage.

3. **Communicate and collaborate with others**

   a. **Know the agenda**—Some people enter a situation without knowing where they're being led. But you need to know in what direction you're being taken if you're to avoid unpleasant surprises. Be ready to maneuver and adjust as you proceed. Understand your objectives and know the meeting attendees. Review and study the agenda. Do some research and ask questions about what the meeting is going to be about so you can prepare yourself accordingly. Industries and markets are constantly (and rapidly) evolving, and to survive, your organization must be maneuverable. To compete effectively, you and your people need to understand the skills that are required to win—speed, agility, and innovation—as the competitive landscape shifts. This maneuver strategy involves building competitive insights, taking valuable positions before competitors recognize them, and attacking competitors in areas of their recognized weakness.

   b. **Know the key players**—Familiarize yourself with the participants involved. This builds the vested interest and gives you time to visualize the participants and tailor your pitch.

3. **Respond versus react**—Normally, the challenge with any crisis involves reaction, but we can't be effective when we approach the unexpected with anxiety and unease. Rather than reacting, we need to be able to respond.

   a. **React**—Reacting is short-sighted, impulsive, spontaneous, and based on emotions, without keeping the result in mind. It can be counterproductive. Never react to emotions with emotions.

   b. **Respond**—Responding is thoughtful, rational, and logical, putting your thoughts before the action. It is productive and requires attentive listening and contemplation in the moment.

continued

4. **Build your conflict-management skills**—If you try to manage conflict, you can ease some of the tension in the moment. Find a way to collaborate with the others involved, offering empathy and positive communication to bring about a better outcome.

5. **Develop your negotiation skills**—See if you can achieve a give-and-take method of exchange during an ambush. Be adaptable and open but act decisively to find a solution that can lead to favorable results.

6. **Keep a positive tone**—In a challenging situation, it can help to be winsome. Engage with others positively. Listen to them, take a genuine interest in what they're saying, find common ground, and make an intentional effort to achieve a win-win situation, which can enable you to get the information and results you want.

7. **Stick to the facts**—To maintain your credibility and avoid conflict, emphasize and stay grounded in facts. Any overexaggeration or fabricated interpretations can lead to multiple unanswered questions and doubts.

8. **Defend yourself**—Stand up for what you believe in with courage. You don't have to let anyone play to your insecurities. Stay calm and assertive. Be authentic and transparent. Take ownership of your feelings and response, and don't let anyone invalidate or override you. This comes with practice and preparation.

9. **Don't be afraid to fight back**—You will need to break down the barriers in your mind and keep moving forward despite your fears. Despite the odds, don't give up the fight. In fact, some of the things that scare you may be the very reason you need to believe in yourself, stick to your guns, and act on your convictions. That provides you with a chance to win.

These moments of conflict can be emotionally charged, but you don't have to give in to the emotions. Consider the story of the Buddha and the gift of anger: Buddha was traveling for many days and stopped at a town to give a speech. During his message, one angry man kept shouting insults and yelling at Buddha for no apparent reason. But Buddha did not acknowledge the man and delivered his speech calmly. This further infuriated the angry man. He came up to Buddha afterward and said, "I have been shouting for so long, and you did not say anything. Why?"

Buddha asked the angry man, "If you give a gift to someone, and they don't accept it, to whom would the gift belong?"

The angry man said, "I am the giver, so it will belong to me."

There is a valuable lesson for all of us here in learning how to deal with angry, negative, or toxic people. If we don't react and don't accept their "gift," instead protecting and saving our energy for positive things, that gift of toxicity will remain with the giver. Ultimately, it hurts them more than it hurts you. When you are ambushed in business, pause and think to buy some time before you respond. Don't engage in a way that throws fuel on the fire. See if you can calmly reduce the flames. Simply look for solutions, find a way forward, and apply the principles we share in this chapter to move beyond the ambush.

Early in Rita's career, while studying for her CPA exam, she got an internship at a local company. She took this opportunity very seriously, always completing her assignments in a timely manner, making sure she was punctual and ready, and assisting others when needed. She thrived in the role and over time was entrusted with greater levels of responsibility. But in the day-to-day, she observed that when she approached other team members to get to know them, see if she could lend them a hand, or collaborate on assignments, they rebuffed her. When she spoke, she noticed eye-rolling. The more she tried to ignore this cold response and continue to help others, the more coldness she received. Eventually, she came to understand that some of her coworkers were behaving like this due to their insecurities, which made her feel unwelcome, and the work environment became so unhealthy that she eventually needed to approach her supervisor for advice. She received no support, and after a while she had to make the difficult decision to leave the internship.

Rita had set out to contribute something meaningful through her internship, and though the negativity she received stung, she decided not to focus on what had happened to her but rather on what she could do moving forward. In the face of rejection and challenge, she chose to learn from the experience and apply her skills at a place where she could make more of a difference. We learned how we could use this unpleasant experience meaningfully to help others.

During our business journey in S&A Consulting Group, we reached out to students fresh out of college who needed to enhance their skills through professional development and internships. We committed ourselves to hiring and training these young professionals, giving them experience in a team environment, training them in the skills they could use later in their life, and showing them what goes into building a company. We mentored the interns in business processes, financials, communications, and project management skills. Today, the interns we invested in are all either well placed in larger consulting companies or running their own businesses.

If you experience a setback, know that you can still change a situation for the better. It may not look like what you'd originally planned, but challenges give us perspective on what's important and allow us to think creatively to find a unique way to add value. A warrior in business will face challenges and disappointment, but they won't stay stuck in it. Look at the challenge full in the face, embrace it, then use it to launch yourself to a better place. An ambush demands a response. Give it a good one.

DON'T JUST SURVIVE, THRIVE

Don't settle for just getting by. Starting and operating a small business is hard enough, but you can only go so far if you stay in survival mode. In certain medical situations, patients are hooked up to monitors that measure their vitals, including their heart rate. Think about the health of your business. Even if you're just barely surviving, you still have a pulse. Survival doesn't look like a flatliner but instead still has a continuous pulse—there's movement. If, as a business, you only work on survival, you're not going to thrive or make it very far. You need to do the things that allow you to become healthy. When you focus on thriving as a business, you bring a vibrant pulse to what you do.

A HEALTHY BUSINESS HAS LIMITLESS POTENTIAL.

In today's competitive world, surviving might get your foot in the door, but for you to excel, you will need to step up to challenges and consistently build a strong mindset—you need to get healthy. What does this look like? Rigorously preparing for what you can, staying aware of opportunities, developing new skills, adopting innovative technology, fostering a supportive team environment, building your resources, creating partnerships and alliances, and being on the lookout for growth potential. Your company can be in reasonable health if you take the right steps, but you still never know when an ailment, a virus, or a health scare might come. You'll need to take the necessary measures to survive these unexpected situations.

Two years into our consulting business, we had a very large project with a Fortune 50 company that composed around 60 percent of our revenue. Everything went fine with the project for a while, but then one day, Nip received a call from the contract administrator telling us the company had decided to stop the project, and our services would no longer be needed. We felt we had been ambushed. Nip sought to understand the reasons because the project had been exceeding expectations. He also asked how the project could be canceled when we had a legally binding agreement. The contract administrator said, "So sue me," and that was the end of our work with this company.

With a sudden loss of 60 percent of our revenue, we had to hike to find other projects and assignments so we could stay in business. We did manage to quickly find new clients, but in doing so, we also learned a couple of valuable lessons for our business model: No work we do for any one particular client should make up more than 20 to 30 percent of our revenue, and we should always have multiple agreements at a time in case anything happens. Also, we agreed that our marketing efforts cannot stop, even when things are going great. Since then, we've gone through tough times here and there, but our learning and growth from that ambush has served us well and allowed us to stay profitable and healthy all these years. In times of ambush, assess the situation and the damage and decide on the next course of action. You can't go back, but you can take action that sets you up to thrive in the future.

We've seen similar things happen to lots of other small companies. One of our clients had a government contract with a big agency in our region, and we encouraged him to look at additional options for his services and products. In addition to that, we had advised this particular client to strengthen his marketing services while he worked on his big government contract, so he had other leads if anything fell through. But he did not listen. When he lost that contract prematurely, he had to file for bankruptcy, lay off all his people, and eventually had to close the business. So, while you give your absolute best to the work you have, to survive an ambush you must look ahead and position yourself well.

Having multiple options for surviving an ambush in business is a good strategy. Small start-ups don't always feel they have time to look at other ways to do business. But you don't want to learn the hard way that you should always have something else ready in your back pocket, whether that's another strategy or another client.

THINK AHEAD TO THRIVE.

Keep your eyes trained on the things you need to do to thrive. Stay focused on your purpose. Don't become unnecessarily distracted by irrelevant details and derail yourself. In our case, we were not only unhappy that our large contract had suddenly been terminated but also that the relationship we'd built had dissolved. But rather than reacting with negative emotions to the unexpected news we'd received, we took a step back and found a response so we could move our business forward more effectively and put safeguards in place for the future. That's the kind of response a warrior in business needs. Think ahead to thrive. Gain an awareness of what your strengths, assets, resources, and opportunities are and then further develop and explore these.

Always be open to multiple perspectives. In the army, a technique for discovering what you don't know is to use the "eyes of the enemy." Military leaders often ask themselves what the enemy is paying attention to, then shift their own attention accordingly to illuminate the potential blind spots and alternative perspectives. The same can be applied to a business and its competitors, your people, customers, and various industries. Ask yourself the following:

- Who is doing well? What market segments are my rivals focused on?

- What products or services are they launching?

- Which customers are exhibiting new behaviors? Which have stayed loyal?

- What are rivals and customers paying attention to?

- Which workplace innovations are taking place in their businesses?

- What new needs are employees responding to?

- What potential opportunities can be extended to employees to further develop their skills?

Use the insights you gain to inform not only the everyday decisions you make today but also the quick decisions you'll need to make in an ambush. Part of thriving also includes surrounding yourself with people who inspire, motivate, and uplift you. As John Maxwell stated, "It's hard to soar like an eagle when you surround yourself with turkeys."

You can pull yourself out of survival mode by adjusting your influences and inspirations. Spend your time and energy on people who make you better.

HOW NOT TO GET AMBUSHED

Finally, the best way to avoid an ambush is to take preventive measures and build safeguards in advance. Consider the following best practices.

Resolve slight differences before they escalate into larger conflicts. The key is not to avoid conflict but to resolve it in a healthy, constructive way and keep your relationships strong and growing. If you approach conflict as an opportunity for growth, then when you successfully resolve conflict in a relationship, it builds trust. Seek support early on and build helpful, positive alliances.

Continuously work on developing relationships to build connection and mutual trust, components that are necessary when you need to improvise during an ambush.

Learn to manage and control your emotions and stay calm, so you're in practice for a sudden situation. Teach yourself not to hit a mental panic button but instead to look for solutions. You can empower yourself to act rather than react. Communication is critical in crisis situations, and what we communicate and how we communicate is important. *Both the context and content are equally important.*

Sometimes there's the option to exit or retreat. Stay calm and know your options will make you confident enough to recognize your value and know when it's time to move on.

Gather the data you need beforehand. Facts will always help you win in an ambush. Later, if you need to make a decision, make sure it's supported by the data.

Appreciate people in your life. There are two ways to pay back your employees: economically and emotionally. It should become second nature to practice recognizing, appreciating, and acknowledging people on a daily basis. By doing this, we have seen how people in our circle and those who worked with us went above and beyond to give their absolute best, irrespective of how much they were paid. Probably more important than taking care of your employees economically is taking care of them emotionally. It doesn't cost any money (or doesn't have to) to make someone feel valued if you are sincere about it. Show your appreciation for their efforts; praise them in front of their peers. Every single person we've hired knows that we would pay them before we paid ourselves.

Keep it simple: Remember and practice the simplest things, like taking notes, being respectful, being clear and concise, repeating back what you heard, and saying "please" and "thank you." Whether in the battlefield or the boardroom, chaos can make the lines of communication break down and tensions rise. Combat this by putting a simple framework and habits in place.

SET YOURSELF UP TO SUCCEED.

Unexpected things will always happen. Despite the ambushes, you should always come out better. Each one is an opportunity. To emerge from an ambush unscathed, you need to be a leader with a resilient mindset to lead yourself and your business forward.

Executive Summary

- **Unexpected challenges present an opportunity** for a warrior in business to show resiliency.

- **Ask for help**—remember, asking for help is not a weakness.

- Develop a **fearless state of mind** that is open and invites positive change in the face of the unknown.

- In turbulent situations, **it's not about the speed but the accuracy of your action** that gets you through.

- **Practice improvisation** to ensure your actions are based on knowledge and experience when the time comes for spontaneous action.

- For your business to survive in the long term, you must **not only survive an ambush but thrive** in the wake of it.

- To survive an ambush, **you first need to look ahead and position** yourself well.

- Surround yourself with people who **inspire, motivate, and uplift** you.

CHAPTER 5

A WARRIOR IN BUSINESS HAS THE COURAGE TO MOVE FORWARD

IN THE ARMY, CULTIVATING RESILIENCE STARTS LONG before a unit ever deploys. A warrior prepares to be mentally tough as part of their training. In much the same way, courage begins in your mind. The courage you need to achieve what's required in battle comes from having a resilient mind, which then gives you the ability to do things you never thought you could do. Whether in battle or in business, a warrior needs to make a conscious choice to face what lies ahead, proceed forward, and act despite fear. This requires courage. Courage is the spirit within us that inspires us to face anything difficult, painful, or dangerous. Courage enables us to be strong, brave, determined, and firm. Courage is what keeps a warrior moving toward an objective and helps them navigate the complex and stressful terrain before them. Without the courage to move forward, they won't be able to advance in the face of a challenge, progress toward their stated goals, or accomplish necessary tasks.

Some people are born braver than others, but the majority must learn—and build—courage as they go along. To develop courage as a business warrior, you need to exercise calmness and mental strength, take risks, choose progress over perfection, and be proactive, willing, and able to embrace change. The courage you can gain by living according to these principles will create a fire in your belly that will keep you moving forward. And when you move forward, you will not only gain ground, but you will also allow yourself to overcome hardship and learn how to tap into unknown possibilities within yourself. So, start practicing moving your business forward, even at the risk of upsetting the status quo. Standing still is not an option.

PROCEED WITH CALMNESS AND STRENGTH

To understand how important and critical calmness and mental strength are to your undertakings, you first need to recognize their tremendous positive impact. Calmness and mental strength create an awareness of your inner self and of your environment, which allows you to observe the big picture in advance, giving you a competitive edge.

The inverse is easy to see. The detrimental effects of an absence of calmness and mental strength include an abundance of negative emotions: aggravated, anxious, edgy, aggressive, fearful, fidgety, frustrated, impulsive, overwhelmed, panicked, restless, shaky, tense, and worried. Any of these emotional states will minimize your ability to manage whatever obstacles you face. You will be unable to overcome difficulties or face up to problems, and you will also struggle with making the right decision at the right time, which may result in negative or unintended consequences, costing you professional relationships, an important project, or—the worst outcome of all—your entire business.

Calmness and mental strength aren't just for tough times; they're also critical for managing stress in everyday life. As your mental strength increases, you'll gain confidence in your ability to deal with whatever problems you face daily. Ask yourself this: Do I really want to be in a state of mind where I feel out of control? Your ability to find courage and move forward to achieve your mission has everything to do with keeping yourself calm and mentally strong. Let's walk through how to be in a state of calmness and mental strength, so you can be at your absolute best.

CALMNESS

If you've ever been stressed or anxious, you've probably noticed the negative energy that rises in your chest, leading you to feel agitated or impulsive. Or you might feel weak inside, like you lack the strength to act. In a stressed or agitated state of mind, the business warrior can easily lose sight of their purpose, main objective, or what's essential. It's important to pull back, refocus your energy, and recalibrate so you don't miss the point, purpose, or opportunity. If you can approach a situation with calmness, you will be in a state of tranquility, giving you a feeling of relaxation or openness and the ability to think about things more clearly. When you're calm, you're not in a reactive mode, so you are able to respond mindfully and proactively with clarity and confidence.

RECALIBRATE SO YOU DON'T MISS THE POINT, PURPOSE, OR OPPORTUNITY.

There are a few daily practices we incorporate into our daily life to achieve a state of calmness in the middle of chaos. Calmness results when there is self-awareness, which means you need to know what causes your anxiety and what you can do to navigate through it. Fundamentally, your mind is blank. Memories and imagination are wonderful gifts, but these gifts pull you from the present moment and make your mind travel, often feeding stress, anxiety, and avoidance.

One way to calm yourself is to breathe deeply. Practicing yoga or mindfulness exercises daily can help with this, especially before you begin your day, even if only for five minutes.

Nip has been very disciplined and practices early every morning by taking twenty to thirty minutes to himself, practicing breathing and mindfulness meditation in a quiet place, away from all distractions, which helps him start his day in a calm and serene state of mind. This has been his habit for years. Even when he is traveling and leaving home at four or five a.m., he makes sure to take five to ten minutes for himself. This has helped him to improve his focus and strengthen his self-awareness. Working on this mindful strategy as a daily routine will relieve stress and support a more balanced approach to your day and thought process by sensing the silence. We surrender. We tune in to self-awareness. It's a practice that invites us to be with ourselves.

Having a consistent routine and finding time to relax can go a long way toward finding balance in our lives. "Down time" can provide the space we need to think through a situation, work through our feelings, or just let us rest.

BEING CALM ALLOWS YOU TO CREATE MORE INFLUENCE.

The more you practice calmness, the more you will become aware of the brave space that resides within you, the space that can hold your emotions and keep them in check. You'll have a better ability to concentrate and analyze a situation more thoroughly, which will help you better determine how to act and make wise decisions. Being calm allows you to create more influence. In a state of calmness, your communication skills will improve, giving you the ability to convey your thoughts impactfully and with strength.

MENTAL STRENGTH

Whatever you seek to become in your life, mental strength is the key to long-term achievement. You need willpower and determination to reach the highest potential. You will always come up against obstacles and challenges; life is not a smooth ride for anyone. But by building mental strength, you can increase your mental muscle, thereby developing resilience against unforeseen risk and hardships.

When you possess mental strength, you can perform at your absolute best and can achieve the following:

- **Think realistically**—This is about regulating your thoughts. Too much optimism or pessimism can result in incorrect judgment and may lead to serious errors. Instead, thinking in a clear and balanced way will give you the ability to control your thoughts, which will improve your judgment of the situation.

- **Control your emotions**—A warrior must control their emotions, or else their emotions will control them. Coping and managing emotions will allow you to avoid getting into arguments, chasing temptation, or reacting impulsively. Mental strength gives you the courage to face your fears because you can trust your ability to deal with anxiety. The more you step out of your comfort zone, the more confidence you'll gain in managing your emotions.

- **Take productive action**—Your mental strength grows stronger when you put your resources, time, and energy into constructive activities. Not only can you learn from your mistakes, but you can also learn to avoid making the same mistake again. This practice will also help you recover from failure and overcome challenges. Mental strength gives us the courage to act despite fear.

Let's define mental strength as mental toughness, which means having courage, confidence, control, commitment, and the ability to face any type of challenge.

Mental toughness is having trust in your abilities, managing your emotions, and having influence over your life. You can power through tasks, seeing them through to completion, and remain resilient to changes, perceiving them as opportunities rather than threats.

To cultivate mental strength, you need to take the same approach you would toward developing physical strength: through regular exercise. You can also build your mental strength by exercising your brain.

What we all need to understand is that mental strength is not something you achieve in one day. It is an ongoing process and there is not one way to achieve or cultivate mental strength. However, it does require cultivating certain habits and steady effort.

Having strong, supportive relationships with others can enhance your mental toughness, so surround yourself with people who encourage and uplift you. As we mention earlier in this book, seek mentors or join groups where you can share experiences and learn from others.

When you are mentally strong, you can overcome setbacks with courage and confidence. With mental strength, a business warrior has the resiliency required to take risks even with their business when called for.

DON'T BE AFRAID TO TAKE RISKS

To take your business to the next level, you need the courage to take risks. Whenever you move forward or take any action, there's always an inherent risk involved. This might be starting a new business or making changes to an existing one. The list of risks you may face along your business journey is endless: launching a new service or product, moving locations, or hiring a new employee. There's risk inherent in all these actions because no matter how much you prepare, you won't always know the outcome or the ripple effects of your actions. This ever-present risk of threat means that the very first step toward growth is often the most difficult to take.

LIKE THE TURTLE, YOU MUST STICK YOUR NECK OUT IF YOU WANT TO MOVE FORWARD.

So how do you muster up courage when walking into the unknown? Recall the example of the turtle. A turtle is unable to move forward unless it sticks its neck out. It must allow its head to emerge from its shell, and it must extend its neck as it takes steps in the direction it wants to go. For the turtle, its natural defense system is to keep its neck tucked in, which is its comfort zone. The turtle must leave its comfort zone and become vulnerable if it ever wants to accomplish any goal, or even just move away from the place where it started.

In much the same way, it takes courage and a willingness to move forward to advance your business. Just like the turtle, you must stick your neck out if you want to move forward. You need to be willing to come out of your comfort zone and muster up the courage to face some risk. Once you do, you can advance to thoughts and actions that are more productive and creative. In our work with clients, we often refer to this as "Turtle Theory." It's a thought exercise that has led our clients to the kind of daring thinking and action that drives success. Turtle Theory is about keeping steady, taking calculated risks, making progress rather than being frozen by the thought of an unachievable goal, and consistently following your mission and purpose to get to the end point.

In Aesop's well-known fable "The Tortoise and the Hare," we find another example of what it takes to make progress toward a goal. The story demonstrates how a tortoise goes from being an unlikely participant in a footrace to becoming its ultimate winner, succeeding by keeping steady and consistent, not giving up until it reaches the finish line. The tortoise's opponent, the hare, demonstrates overconfidence in his ability that costs him the race. In a business environment, you don't have to be the loudest, fastest, or showiest competitor to reach your goal. You don't have to take the biggest risks, find shortcuts, or be the most aggressive to accomplish your mission. Whatever pace you set, steadiness and persistence *can* win the race. What matters most is the courage to enter the race and your level of focus and consistency. If, like the tortoise, you don't give up, you will get there.

An added benefit of steadiness is that it creates harmony and reduces pressure. When you are proceeding cautiously and not rushing to achieve results, your approach will lead to a sense of calmness, not panic. In the corporate world, people always seem pressured to achieve certain results. How many times have you seen business leaders rushing, making themselves and the people who work for them stressed, angry, or upset when they're faced with the urgency to achieve results? The pressure to compete and succeed is so intense that everyone looks for shortcuts and instant gratification.

Nip once had a colleague who, as part of a continuing contract, needed to deliver parts to the Department of Defense. On one occasion, he had the parts ready and there was an urgency to send them, but one of the established steps in the process had not been completed. This colleague gave the go-ahead to his team to circumvent the process. He shipped what was needed on time and made his quota. But the truth later came out after an investigation, and the colleague and his whole team lost their jobs. He could easily have waited a couple of days, but his sense of pressure to compete and succeed wound up costing him his career, and he was unable to be hired elsewhere in the industry. The pressure to achieve came at a great cost in this case.

To work sustainably and effectively, you need to focus on the long-term viability of your business and career instead of focusing exclusively on short-term goals, such as this quarter's deliverables. This approach may seem contrary to the typical way of doing business. But when you allow yourself to focus on long-term goals, you can achieve growth over the long haul, which is ultimately an investment in the stability of your business.

Part of that long-term focus must be centered on future growth and change. Your business cannot become what you want it to be if you continue doing the same things you always do. If you hold on to what you are, you will never have new revelations, innovations, or change—no transformation will ever take place. You must be like flowing water and not become stagnant. Stagnant water is damaging. It attracts bugs and mosquitos, grows algae, and eventually decay sets in. To avoid this, you must stay fluid and productive, and that requires action on your part. Forward motion is the answer. However, it is your choice to make.

PROGRESS, NOT PERFECTION

There's a fine line between striving for excellence and getting sucked into a perfectionist sinkhole. In typical American corporate environments, business leadership's focus is on perfection and results. Their metric for success has become purely a numbers game. If, instead, you can approach your business with a "progress, not perfection" mindset, it will demonstrate that you recognize all the efforts you and your team are putting into your organization and truly feel proud and appreciative. Being able to celebrate your achievements irrespective of the volume of the results is a rejection of perfectionist ideology and the more insidious effects it can have on your business.

Perfectionism is the enemy of progress. When you aim for perfection, you are bound to struggle with restlessness because you will become obsessed with the idea of making your decisions and actions "perfect" and "right." This happens because perfectionism presents a false binary: either all or nothing. The truth is that progress often means small and simple progress now, which iterates and evolves over time to become stronger and better. With those priorities in mind, you will gain courage because you will be strong and powerful inside. Striving for perfection will drain you emotionally, leaving you and your team stressed. If, instead, you work toward sustainable improvement, you will feel happy about where your progress has taken you. Without the pressure of perfectionism, you will see it's not about making the "right" choice all the time, as long as you're making a decision and moving forward with it. This progress will lead to confidence because you will be able to track your progress. As you focus on progression, you will find strengths and weaknesses and learn how to overcome barriers.

PERFECTIONISM IS THE ENEMY OF PROGRESS.

When you are on this journey, you are bound to see things go wrong. You cannot stay stuck in your failures. You must examine the options, alternatives, and creative ways at your disposal to overcome your problems. You must ask yourself, What is the next right move? By answering this question, you will be directing your brain and heart to search for a productive and courageous answer. Unbound by the strictures of perfectionism, you can achieve progress.

Many of us had to unlearn our perfectionist tendencies during the early days of the COVID lockdown. Adjusting to the new norm of sometimes working from home or shopping and working online was the kind of drastic change no one had envisioned for themselves. But those who were able to thrive during this time stayed flexible and remained open to change in a positive way. They found the new habits and routines could enrich the way they worked. They realized that these new obstacles didn't dictate that they wouldn't reach their goals; instead, they saw that their circumstances still allowed for joy, perspective, and harmony on the journey to their objectives, as long as they were able to let go of perfectionism. In this way, their lives became more fulfilling. They were able to appreciate the beauty of the journey more than they craved crossing the finish line.

Many people will not even try to act on a new idea, because they fear not achieving perfection. To make progress, you can't stress yourself out with the discomfort of potential setbacks or failure. At least some degree of failure is unavoidable for everyone. Just start over again. A warrior in business knows they must grow, or else they will deteriorate. The essence of all growth is in one's willingness to change for the better. Old attitudes of all or nothing must be abandoned if you want to move forward and make progress. Focusing on the false binary of failure or success can ultimately drive you to failure.

BE PROACTIVE AND TAKE INITIATIVE

Building a foundation of courage and mental strength allows a warrior to be proactive and to take initiative. Being proactive and taking the initiative are, of course, two key attributes not only in war but also in the competitive world of business we live in. When a warrior in business is proactive, they anticipate needs and challenges so they and their team are prepared to overcome them. You cannot anticipate all challenges, but being proactive will make you confident in your ability to foresee and plan for potential obstacles. As the saying goes, "An ounce of prevention is worth a pound of cure." Whether they are on a battlefield or off duty, warriors must be proactive thinkers. It is what allows them a modicum of control in uncertain circumstances. It grants them more awareness of their situation, allowing them to jump at opportunities when they present themselves.

TAKING INITIATIVE MEANS RISKING OWNING AN IDEA THAT MAY NOT WORK.

In times of war, taking initiative might mean sending scouts out to survey the site of a future battle, or studying the enemy's movements in previous skirmishes. In business, taking initiative means working on something beyond the scope of your job description—proposing a new direction, a new idea, or a new intervention, even if it means you are risking failure. Taking the initiative involves running the risk of owning an idea that may not work.

Showing initiative has become increasingly important in today's environment. Organizations want employees who can think on their feet and act without waiting for someone to tell them what to do. When you are a proactive thinker who takes initiative, you become resilient and will develop a growth mindset. This comes from your willingness to go beyond what people expect of you and to do more than what you have been asked. You have the courage to lead the project, solve the problems, and not dwell on the past. This type of flexibility, attitude, and courage is what pushes teams and organizations to innovate and overcome the competition, instead of missing out on opportunities.

When you take the initiative, you are bound to face setbacks, unimaginable hurdles, and difficulties. In those situations you will need resilience and persistence to achieve what you are setting out to do. You must not feel paralyzed by the thought of failure, whether it involves yourself or another team member. *The organization must have patience to deal with failure because that's a necessary part of the process.* This tolerance for failure must be built into the culture of the organization and viewed as growth rather than penalty. That doesn't mean that if somebody acts irresponsibly, you should just let it go. Instead, use moderation and perspective when considering all the facts, and you will be able to figure out the best course of action.

DISRUPT THE STATUS QUO

Courageous action disrupts the status quo. If you want something new, different, unique, or innovative, you must be prepared to choose disruption, and you must choose change. As human beings, we don't like change or disruption. We all resist disruption because change necessitates flexibility to adapt to new norms. When we know new challenges may occur, our minds start spinning and we feel out of control. But the truth is that your business will not last long if you don't have the courage to try something new. This is of the utmost importance: You must opt into disruption if you want your business to thrive.

YOU MUST CHOOSE DISRUPTION
IF YOU WANT YOUR BUSINESS TO THRIVE.

In today's changing world, you have a choice to either adhere to the status quo—which will ultimately result in collapse—or you can lead or join the disruption. If you choose the latter, it is likely to result in the reinvention of your business and, potentially, your industry as a whole. Disruption teaches you a lesson, which tells a story of how things that seem will last forever often come to be short-lived. We still remember early on in our business when we could not do without fax machines and floppy disks. Look what has happened now: Fax machines are rarely used, and floppy disks no longer exist. Those functions are now accomplished by new technologies like email, texts, and other internet-based systems. We can get the information we need from anywhere in the world with access through the internet. We used to have long rows of filing cabinets, but today, all our files and data are cloud-based, which enables us to access our files remotely We used to have giant printers in our office, but we've embraced new technological innovations and have adapted to grow with the times. We not only rid ourselves of frustrating paper jams but also saved time, money, hassle, and physical space in the office by moving away from the status quo. And we achieved more efficiency in the process!

Do-or-Die: Case Studies in Unwise Risk Aversion

Not embracing disruption can have disastrous consequences for your business. Consider the unenviable fates of these three corporate giants, all household names in the past.

- **Sears**—With its huge inventory, Sears dominated its competition for years. In its day, it was almost an Amazon of sorts. But unfortunately, its leadership did not have the foresight to adopt newer technology and allow disruption to lead the way, which would have allowed the company to make the necessary transitions to carry it into a new era. As a result, its products and services became irrelevant to customers. Sears, once a US retail powerhouse, has now shut down most of its operations.

- **Kodak**—Kodak invented the digital camera back in 1975 but did not invest in the technology, ultimately blowing its opportunity to lead the digital photography revolution. Because the company remained so focused on its film-processing business—which was immensely popular with consumers at the time—it did not foresee the changes that would happen. Kodak filed for bankruptcy in 2012.

- **Blockbuster**—Blockbuster was a titan in the video rental space. When Netflix made an offer to buy Blockbuster back in 2000 for fifty million dollars, Blockbuster, set in its own way of doing things, turned the offer down. Today, Blockbuster is bankrupt, while Netflix is worth more than one hundred billion dollars.

The moral of these stories is either do or die. Warriors in business need to lead the way and embrace disruption. And they must approach this with the understanding that not every change is going to be positive.

Back in 2008, our business, S&A Consulting Group, was in that place. When we were all facing the financial crisis as a nation, our company was planning to buy a building because our lease payments were a huge expense to maintain in a diminishing market. We looked at our business model, the market, growing technology, and how we were serving our clients in the USA and beyond. Being in the consulting business, we envisioned being able to run much of our business from anywhere, if we implemented new technology. We concluded after reviewing with our team that we did not want to be tied to a space and didn't require large offices in various places to conduct our business. We decided to let the idea of purchasing a building go.

Instead of purchasing a building for our office space, we decided to build a home office. Home-based businesses were not considered a particularly good option during those years. We took the risk, embraced disruption, and decided to move our offices to our home. Most of our employees became independent contractors and started working remotely. Many people at that time thought we'd gone out of business, but that was not the case. In fact, we have been running a profitable, successful, and growing business for the past thirty-plus years. The truth was that we were able to foresee what was coming and adapted to change instead of supporting the status quo with huge monthly rental payments, which would have added to our overhead. By adopting new technology, we could serve our clients from anywhere in the world. Now, we can be in our home office and take a visual tour of a client's industrial process or conduct our meetings with consultants and clients all over the world.

Consider also how the COVID pandemic shook the world and forced everyone—from Fortune 50 company employees to small businesses—to work from home. Now these same people say we were smart to make the shift to remote work fifteen years back. The transition of moving from a large office space to a home office environment was not easy. It took several months to carefully craft this change and to position and prepare our people for the transition. We were not just changing space or equipment; we had employees and some independent consultants to factor in as well. We made sure during this transition that our people were taken care of while going through this adjustment, so our workforce was positioned in such a way that there was no negative impact on their lives and families.

IT'S DO-OR-DIE IF YOU WANT TO MOVE FORWARD.

Interestingly, when COVID hit during 2020, we had extraordinarily little interruption to our business because we were already set up and operating smoothly from our home office. We added more technology, and we were able to serve our clients 24/7, being there for them in challenging times. Again, business owners and leaders need to lead the disruption. It's do-or-die if you want to move forward, stay relevant, and be at the top of your game.

TAKE RESPONSIBILITY

Moving forward requires the courage to take responsibility and ownership. We cover ownership, responsibility, and accountability in an earlier chapter, but here we focus on the deeper meaning of responsibility and what it looks like to transition into a mindset of ownership, which gives a business warrior the ability to respond with toughness and be empowered to act. We don't see ownership as a physical possession but rather a strength, asset, and driving force that compels the warrior to think things through and prepares them to conquer the world.

In the military, the best fighters and leaders are those who not only follow through with their responsibilities and assignments but also go above and beyond. They take ownership and initiative and lead their teams to victory. They don't limit themselves to the basic duties—doing only what's required. They hold themselves to profound responsibility, facing every challenge with honor, courage, and commitment. They make no excuses and fix problems as they arise. They don't play the victim but instead do heroic acts. All of us can do heroic acts. And if you want to be a warrior in business, it is a prerequisite.

There is so much to learn from the life of a warrior. Whenever a warrior decides to do something, they go all in, taking responsibility for what they do. They understand why they are doing it, and then they proceed with their actions. They are not doubtful because they know what's needed from them. They are prepared to sacrifice and even give their own life for the sake of the mission. They don't blame others for their actions.

You can implement the same attitude in your work. Taking ownership is everyone's responsibility, not just the person or people who own the company. It is a collective-thinking approach. It can be detrimental when employees blame and make excuses rather than stepping in, following through, and going above and beyond. In business and in everyday life, you cannot point fingers and call others out, thinking it's everyone else's fault but your own. Blame and excuses shift responsibility to other people and send the message that you are powerless and vulnerable. You will lose your ability to change anything around you. You'll waste time and energy, become insecure, and fail to act. Again, focus on what is within your control—your effort, your response, your determination, your desire to excel, and your decision to act.

The ultimate responsibility lies on your shoulders and not on anyone else's. It starts and ends with you. A warrior needs to be in control of the situation and their ego. They look within. They understand that the solutions lie with them. You are the commander of your work, so take courageous ownership and lead by example. Start with small steps. As you gain ground, your courage will grow gradually. You will have the ability and mindset to move faster and accomplish bigger and more daunting tasks. Great things don't happen on impulse; they result from a series of small things connected together to create something great.

Encourage and demonstrate responsibility to yourself and to the people around you. As a child, you were likely told to make your bed daily, straighten things in your room, and do your homework. It is about assuming and accepting that we are responsible for our life and actions until what needs to be done becomes a habit, a discipline. The road will be hard, and you will be asked to solve tough problems, but there is a deeper meaning to it. We need to constantly feed and build our minds with this notion that it is you who is the ultimate driver of your destiny, and you have the power to rise above your problems and help others do the same. Leaders who don't realize this don't last long in business. Don't let anything paralyze or incapacitate you; instead, make every effort to overcome the hardships. In time, you'll see no matter how trying a situation is, nothing can truly weigh you down.

When you find that you're hesitating to move forward, remember, don't just look at your inadequacies or weaknesses. Take inventory of your own skills and your team's skills. Identify your strengths and think about what you have to offer. By taking a step, you can gain more skills so you can beat the odds. It's not that you must ignore your weaknesses or overlook the gaps; it's that you have the power to work on improvement and drive the outcome.

One of the most celebrated painters of the nineteenth century, Vincent van Gogh, confronted numerous challenges in his life but applied courage, commitment, and consistency to amplify his own voice and be himself in a world that was trying to make him something else. Ironically, in spite of the value placed on his art today, he was not able to sell a single painting during his lifetime. One hundred years after his death, his *Portrait of Dr. Gachet* sold for $82.5 million. Van Gogh once said, "What would life be if we had no courage to attempt anything?" Life would lack beauty, creativity, and meaning.

The list goes on. If Steve Jobs didn't have the courage to attempt and create, there would be no MacBook. If the Wright brothers did not muster the courage to invent, design, and develop, we wouldn't be where we are with airplanes today. If you do not invite and engage in new encounters and experiences, you will never gain new perspectives.

Ownership is not a one-time consideration. It should be a lifelong commitment to ourselves and to our employees. It is an individual reflection during which we ask ourselves the tough questions to keep ourselves accountable. It's a habit, and we continue to give our absolute best as we practice it until it becomes part of our routine. Then it becomes a shared value with our teams. When you take true ownership and responsibility in your work, you will never lose sight of your purpose, and your actions and behavior will be aligned with your mission. Plus, you will perform better under pressure during tough situations.

We need to develop a warrior mindset and learn how to grow from pain, setbacks, failures, obstacles, challenges, losses, and all the tough times in business. In every instance, you have a choice to make: Are you going to be a warrior or a victim? Only one of these builds a successful business and moves forward in a way that brings resiliency. We believe courage is a resilient state of mind. It prepares you to tackle adversity in spite of fears and barriers.

DEVELOP YOUR SENSE OF COURAGE

In business, courage is required of you every day. You can get ahead of difficult situations by identifying current fears that may be keeping you from making progress in your work. When you have strong self-awareness, you can preemptively do something in advance to set yourself up to manage things better. You have options, the power to make choices in your favor, the ability to perform bravely and heroically.

COURAGE, MENTAL STRENGTH, AND RESILIENCE COME FROM MAINTAINING FOCUS ON WHAT'S MOST IMPORTANT TO YOU.

Courage, mental strength, and resilience come from maintaining focus on what's most important to you. When you are aligned with your purpose, you have more clarity about what to do. When you are more certain about what you want to achieve, you know better how you are going to achieve it. When you achieve a single purpose, you can be more fearless and daring.

Warrior Alignment Exercise

As a warrior in business, it is essential that you stay aligned with your purpose, maintaining your focus on what really matters and allowing distractions to fall away. To ensure you are acting in alignment with your own purpose, make a habit of reflecting on the following:

- Who you are
- Why you are in business
- What your purpose in life is
- What your purpose in *business* is
- What your ultimate goal is and what you want to achieve
- What motivates you
- What demotivates you

Remember, you don't have to do it all alone. You can be purposeful about creating meaningful relationships. You will be able to face challenges with more strength, ingenuity, and perseverance if you know you have a supportive team with you. The better the relationships you form, the more resilient you're going to be because you will have the wisdom of others and a support network to fall back on if you need it. Your connections can make an enormous difference in helping you move bravely ahead. Lean on those relationships. Sticking together during tough times will make things easier, and crossing into uncharted territory with others will make you stronger. Foster deeper, more meaningful relationships instead of superficial acquaintances. Seek out people who can inspire and motivate you. Surround yourself with the company of winners and big thinkers.

To be a warrior in business, you must increase your capacity for courage by cultivating a calm and strong mindset; focusing on your purpose; prioritizing progress over perfectionism; taking initiative; and embracing disruption, change, and the risks as they occur. Also remember that a business warrior's life and mission is full of potential. You have everything to gain. If you can live with a mindset of abundance, you will be able to see your own growth in a positive light and stay aligned with your purpose, eschewing petty distractions. In the end, a warrior proceeds no matter what. They rely on the support of others, but they also know they're there to do their own absolute best. You only need to live up to your own standards, and you can face tough times if you approach them with courage. Don't be burdened by self-consciousness or others' perceptions of the actions you take to move your business forward. Like the turtle, to make progress, you must stick your neck out and make yourself vulnerable—because without that forward motion, you risk stagnation and failure. As long as you have a pulse, muster the courage to keep going as far as you can.

Executive Summary

- **Courage creates resilience** and helps you adapt to emotional and physical challenges.

- Cultivate **calmness and mental strength** to see the big picture, giving you an advantage over the competition.

- When you're calm, you can **respond mindfully and proactively** with clarity and confidence.

- Mental strength is the key to **long-term achievement and reaching your highest potential**.

- **Risk is inherent in growth**, but that risk can make it difficult to take the first step.

- Turtle Theory states that **to move your business forward, you must stick out your neck**.

- **Steady progress toward your goals** is the only sustainable path to long-term success.

- **Perfectionism is the enemy of progress**—progress, not perfection.

- Taking the initiative involves **running the risk of owning an idea that may not work**.

- You must **either embrace disruption or face extinction**.

CHAPTER 6

A WARRIOR IN BUSINESS NEVER QUITS

WHEN A SOLDIER GOES INTO BATTLE, THERE are two outcomes: favorable or unfavorable. Long before they set foot on the battlefield, the soldier has been tactically trained and prepared to bring about a favorable outcome. Their eyes are trained on the prize, and they're poised to take the actions that will bring them victory. This outcome is their purpose, and it gives them an aim and intent that motivates and drives what they do. As a result, no matter how tough a battle is, the warrior never quits. Trained soldiers learn to endure and overcome the adversity facing them in service of their goal. Their training keeps them focused on the mission, staying the course and seeing things through. Even when faced with setbacks, they calculate their losses while still moving forward toward their objective.

To be a successful warrior in business, you, too, need to develop a never-quit attitude that allows you to accomplish what's needed in the face of whatever obstacles come your way. To be resilient, you must adopt the mindset that quitting is not an option if you want to persevere, keep your business strong, and push it to the next level. Once you know what you're after, you will be able to focus your efforts on making it happen, and this will become the driving force behind your actions. You will recognize that the success of your business and the livelihood of others depend on your ability to push toward the goal in the face of challenges and persevere.

EXPECT ADVERSITY

As part of real life, everyone gets knocked down from time to time. None of us are exempt, but when you're leading a small business, it can feel like the odds are especially stacked against you. Adversity comes in many forms, both big and small. It happens when you don't get the contract you need, when one of your new ventures fail, when your initiative doesn't produce the kind of results you expected, or anytime you lose money on a project. Things can change in the blink of an eye when you run a small business, and these circumstances can leave you feeling frustrated, angry, anxious, and even hopeless. But remember that getting knocked down is part of life and being in business. Just like life, business is not glorious sunshine and rainbows all the time. The adversity you will face will knock you down permanently if you let it. The choice is yours.

REMEMBER THAT GETTING KNOCKED DOWN IS PART OF BEING IN BUSINESS.

You don't need to fear adversity. Instead, learn to expect it, and prepare yourself to take it on so you're ready when tough situations arise. When you anticipate that anything can go wrong at any given time, you're prepared. In our work, we see this every day. Many of our clients don't realize the importance of continuous self-development. They simply hope things continue to go well. But those who don't do the necessary work are knocked down and have a tough time getting back up.

Although external obstacles and challenges are real, the true battle isn't the world against you. It's you against yourself. It's a mental game, and maintaining a no-quit attitude has everything to do with mindset. Upon reflection, you will find that you begin to look for ways you can change yourself in a circumstance. You can't control everything on the outside, but you can be in control of yourself, and having the right mindset makes all the difference when it comes to persevering in what you do.

So, what do you do when you get knocked down flat on your face? At the same moment it happens, you must find the strength to get right back up. What is important is your willingness to persevere and do something about the situation. Perseverance comes from having the right mindset. When you tap into your mental toughness, you'll gain the ability and the strength to not only overcome challenges in your day-to-day grind but also perform under situations of extreme pressure. Even when you take a hit, keep finding your internal strength and resilience not to quit.

HOLD STEADY

Many times, life will test your physical, mental, and emotional resilience. Imagine this scenario: You are starting a business and partnering with another person. You have decided to lease office space, purchase the equipment needed, and hire employees. You are investing and incurring the massive costs that will create a lot of initial overhead.

But then one day, your partner gives you the shocking news that they are leaving you in the middle of a crisis. They tell you they are not going to be able to continue, because they feel fearful and not ready to take that risk. They may not be willing to face the day-to-day challenges needed to create a successful business. You may feel stunned, saddened to lose your business partner, but you know you cannot quit. You must find the strength and determination to continue without them.

Instead of panicking or accepting defeat, take an inventory of your strengths and skills, what you feel you have to offer, what your goals are, and what value you can add to people's lives. Get out and engage in self-development and relationship-building, meet with current and prospective clients, and things will begin to shape up.

When we started our business, we had no clients and had many setbacks. But we did what we are encouraging you to do: We invested in ourselves and our relationships and traveled to new and unfamiliar places to meet with prospective clients. We knocked on doors, made cold calls, woke early each day, and sometimes worked through the night. We were encouraged by our mission and kept a positive, resilient mindset. Our work and commitment paid off. Today, after thirty-plus years of not just surviving but thriving in our business, we have clients on several continents and are still growing and helping our clients succeed. It took perseverance, hard work, sleepless nights, and countless sacrifices to make it to where we are today. But amid the turbulent times, we bounced back, and we remain strong. Most important, our work aligned with our life's purpose of serving others.

FAILURE CAN BE A GREAT STEPPING STONE TO LEARNING.

Resilience requires courage, grit, creativity, and the determination to succeed. At times, you'll encounter people or competitors who don't want you to succeed. Don't let them get into your head. Stay true to your goals and don't be discouraged. You can't control what others think or do, but you can decide how you deal with the situation yourself. If you let others keep you down, you'll never be able to accomplish what's needed. Don't let any circumstance or individual keep you down. It may change the factors at play and alter your original trajectory, but you have the power and agency to assess, reevaluate, adjust as needed, and take action. When things don't work out, keep steady and look for the good. Failure can be a great stepping stone to learning if we objectively review the failure in detail. It can build your character in ways that would have been impossible had you not faced adversity and risen above it.

So how can you take the challenges you face, turn them into something positive and transformative, and keep going? How can you get back up when so many things seem stacked against you? It's your mindset that can change the results. When you're knocked down, it's essential to take some time to regroup. When you get up again, remember what's at stake, play better, and outsmart your opponents. Don't let failures or setbacks dominate or take over your life. What matters is how you approach them. There is a way out, and you have the power to act. Enter any situation with your mindset ready. Start by committing to the task before you and be determined to turn things around.

Getting Back Up

When you find you've run up against a new obstacle or encountered an unexpected setback, take the necessary time to

- Regroup your thoughts.
- Break your problems down into smaller components.
- Prepare your resources.
- Build partnerships and alliances.
- Nurture collaborations with strong bonds.

continued

- Learn or brush up on key skills.
- Make an action plan.
- Reinvent or rebrand your products and services.

As you do all this, stay confident. When you recognize that failures or setbacks can change your course of action into something entirely positive and new, you can achieve surprising and remarkable results.

Corporate giants like Google, Apple, and Amazon experienced failure too, but they each still managed to revolutionize their industries by learning from past mistakes, changing the circumstances, and figuring out how to stay innovative and cutting-edge as businesses. Small businesses don't have the same kinds of resources as large companies do, but the concept is the same. When faced with seemingly insurmountable obstacles, small-business leaders can still come back with breakthrough ideas, rebuild what's broken, and land on results that ultimately drive their growth.

Building your mindset and strength for perseverance involves the following:

- **Assessing your current skills**—Self-awareness is important. A chain is only as strong as its weakest link, so where are your current areas of weakness? Assess and evaluate your professional skills, identifying the gaps that might prevent you from performing your job to the best of your ability. Gauge what's needed to put together an approach to filling the gaps. You might need to learn something via training and professional development. Or you may need to hire people who can manage the things you struggle with. Alternatively, you may need to adjust your systems and approaches to ensure there isn't an obvious weak area. It's important to stay up to date on the needs of your businesses and clients to ensure you're meeting those needs. Even as time passes, continually train and develop your skills, sharpening yourself and learning new techniques. When you feel more competent and capable in needed areas, you gain confidence in your ability to bring about a successful outcome.

- **Not losing yourself in loss**—Losing or feeling defeated is not the end of the world. Highs and lows are always going to be part of the process, part of the game. Failures and setbacks are a necessary part of the learning process, and they provide a chance for improvement. Think of losing as a necessary part of your journey, and don't be discouraged. Through times of hardship, you'll build your resilience muscle and mental and emotional strengths. You might lose at times, but it's only insurmountable if you lose *yourself* as well. Be willing to give 100 percent of yourself or more, so you know you've done your absolute best. Drive the outcome.

- **Remaining poised under pressure**—Calm yourself and keep your emotions under control. In the wake of a failure, you don't need to blame yourself or others. Negative self-talk and thinking will destroy your confidence. Instead, show compassion and grace toward yourself. Adopting this mindset will allow you to view challenges, adversity, trauma, tragedy, and threats more objectively and, in turn, you will feel more in charge of your life. Regroup by summoning your courage and being willing to move ahead. It might be difficult, but consider the time and investment you've already put into your business. You don't have to withdraw, because really, you don't have a choice. Remain poised and think about how you can reinvest your time and efforts.

- **Telling yourself to keep going**—When you feel stuck, one of the best things you can do is to take action. When you increase your actions, you increase the opportunities before you. It can be a game changer when you're able to *do* something about the situation you're in. In a battle, a warrior needs to continue to get up and fight back. When they do, they're not succumbing to defeat. In football, the most successful players practice every day, honing their skills. Practice, practice, and practice. Improve yourself so that you are at your strongest when you take action and seek to change the game. Also, remember that in some cases taking no action is the perfect action.

- **Coaching yourself**—External action is needed to overcome challenges, but so is internal action. Coaching yourself calls for you to reflect on your thoughts, feelings, and perceptions and create greater self-awareness. This allows you to tap into what you need and begin to develop the kind of internal toughness that leads to resiliency. Manage your inner domain by taking the time to dig deep inside yourself. Ask yourself what you want to be about, think about the potential before you, and recognize that you can do whatever you set your mind to. Do this so you can learn to trust and listen to yourself and your gut feelings. Your inner voice is important because it is connected to your intuition, which helps drive decision-making.

Understand that there is a battle within you and know how to get past internal conflicts. These can incapacitate you, making you focus on fear or insecurity, and keep you from taking action. Don't become your own worst enemy. Instead, do all you can to get past internal conflicts. If someone or something opposes you or forces you to take a different direction, look within yourself, stay calm, and seek a solution. If the situation allows, consult with a coach or mentor who can give you an outside perspective and help to remove those conflicting emotions. Step back and review the entire situation.

In his book *Good to Great*, business expert Jim Collins says, "Greatness is not a function of circumstance. Greatness, it turns out, is largely a matter of conscious choice."[4] It's your *choice* to get up and keep fighting. Greatness doesn't just happen by itself. It's an act of will, requiring tireless

----

4   Jim Collins, *Good to Great: Why Some Companies Make the Leap and Others Don't* (New York: Harper Business, 2001).

work and endless determination. It commands you to focus your mind on what's important, then take the necessary action.

A long time ago, a king had many elephants, which he sent into battle, where they won him many wars. One particular elephant was very powerful, skillful, and victorious. It would march into battle to the sound of drums and was considered the strongest of all. Over time, the elephant got older and could no longer go to war. When, one day, it went to a nearby river to drink some water, its feet got stuck in the mud, and it began to sink deeper and deeper. It was sure to meet its demise because, as a huge creature, the elephant was unable to get itself out of the mud. The king and all the villagers who had gathered made every effort to help the elephant out, but nothing worked. Everyone felt helpless to rescue the sinking elephant, which continued to struggle against the rising mud.

But a wise man from the king's court came by, and after assessing the situation, he recommended that someone play the battle drums, the sound the elephant used to hear when it would go into battle. As soon as the troubled elephant heard the battle drums, there was a change in its gestures, behavior, and determination. The sound of the drums brought the elephant back to times when it had to push through to achieve victory. It stood up and started to move. To everyone's astonishment, it pulled itself out of the mud. The elephant surely would have died, but because it was able to tap into its resilient mindset and sense of determination, it was able to extract itself from the mud and go on to live a good life.

So, there was no lack of physical ability in the elephant, only the need to infuse enthusiasm within. The moral of the story is that once we become complacent, we forget the survival skills. We get sucked into the situation of not acting. Each of us needs those battle drums as a reminder that our own act of willpower can pull us out of any circumstances. No matter how helpless or despairing a situation may seem, don't let it overshadow your thinking. To maintain enthusiasm in life, it is necessary to retain a firm, decisive, and purposeful mindset and not let despair control you.

KNOW WHEN TO GO BACK TO THE BASICS

A warrior must have a plan. When they get up after being knocked down, they need to know what to do and how to execute on that. Each failure is a learning opportunity, and no opportunity can be wasted. To know what to do next, they must be able to return to the basics of their training, evaluate what happened, and build from there. In a similar way, when you're trying to prevail over challenging times, it might be necessary for you to go *back to the basics*. This phrase can mean different things for different people and is also sometimes overused. For our purposes, going back to the basics requires questioning and assessing, with the goal of then coming to a solution. But it doesn't mean returning to the start, as if you need to rebuild from scratch, creating a whole new foundation. When you are seeking to overcome adversity, you have an opportunity to look at what you had and take it from there, *refining* it. There is a significant difference between starting from the beginning and doing things completely differently as you move forward with the new knowledge you've obtained about yourself and your circumstances as the result of your setback.

Going back to the basics requires asking yourself questions about what didn't work right this time. A failure might occur because someone didn't deliver, or a system or process didn't function correctly. Examine the whys or whats to see what needs to be done differently. In manufacturing, Nip's area of expertise, when a process doesn't work, he asks the stakeholders to look back at all the major and minor steps. Together, they examine the process, known in his industry as "man, materials, machine." They review each component and then devise a new plan. Once the plan is in place, they then get up from where they were knocked down and execute it with their team.

Going back to basics is returning or sticking to your roots, taking a step back to give yourself some space and time to review and analyze. It is reassessing your business to attain more clarity. For example, you may need to reexamine your marketing to see if you are targeting or reaching out to the right audience. Or check if there is a consistent message in your material that really addresses the pain points of your prospective clients. It is more important than ever to seek a specialist in your field to help navigate you through this process.

Going back to basics is important because by saying, "I already know this" or "This is very basic," we actually shut down our brains from taking in anything new. Having an attitude of openness will free you from preconceptions and you will be able to see, absorb, and learn faster. Learn like a beginner. Going back to the basics doesn't mean you are a failure. Since starting our business, we've constantly been evolving and changing.

A back-to-basics strategy is what allows the warrior in business to move forward. Soldiers are always marching forward as a unit or team. Going back to basics and examining what went wrong will help you keep moving from point A to point B until you make the progress you prepared for. Oftentimes, when our earlier efforts don't work, forward movement requires more investment of time and money, so keep in mind the financial situation of your company, of course. You'll need to make a call about what and how much you're able to invest to keep moving forward.

IN BUSINESS, YOU'RE GOING TO SUCCEED OR FAIL— BUT WITH THE RIGHT MINDSET, YOU WIN EITHER WAY.

DON'T FEAR FAILURE

You'll be met with failure at various points throughout your career. That's a given in business. But it's only when you give up that failure can truly take hold. If you don't want to fail, don't go into business. Albert Einstein has been credited with saying, "You never fail until you stop trying." Similarly, when things don't go your way, keep trying and you won't stay stuck in failure for too long. Repeatedly in business, you'll find yourself up against two outcomes. It's like flipping a coin: You're for sure going to get heads or tails. In business, you're going to succeed or fail—but with the right mindset, you win either way. You'll either achieve success or you'll turn your failure into success. A warrior in business always enters battle with this in mind.

Sometimes, we feel like quitting because we're struggling with self-doubt. A warrior must get out of this kind of thinking. Self-doubt starts with negative feelings. You may linger on regrets, asking what-ifs, beating yourself up, wishing you had done things differently. That's normal. But nevertheless, you must get up. A warrior knows there's no place for self-doubt, because you can't change the past. You can only change the present to reach an attainable outcome in the future.

To overcome self-doubt, you must see beyond the negative and redirect your gaze toward something more productive. Self-doubt affects your communication in whatever you do, blocking your ability to effectively communicate with your teammates and clients. If you continue to focus on how poorly you did or how poorly things went, you won't be able to assess and act. When this happens, seek to understand the situation, being objective in your approach, and communicate the situation at hand to others. That's what will keep you from getting stuck and not getting help. If you find yourself in this place, you may feel like quitting, but it doesn't have to be like that. Having the right mindset and the right thinking can change this, bringing the right actions that keep you going.

Achieving Greatness in the Wake of Failure

Many people who are household names today came to their success only after many setbacks.

- **Michael Jordan**—One of basketball's all-time greats was cut from his high-school basketball team, but that didn't stop him from continuing with what he loved, working hard, and achieving a place of distinction in sports history.

- **Mark Cuban**—This American businessperson, investor, entrepreneur, and TV personality at one time worked as a bartender, but he had bigger dreams. He went on to become a billionaire, co-owner of the Dallas Mavericks, and star on the hit TV series *Shark Tank*.

- **Harrison Ford**—Until his midthirties, Ford worked as a carpenter, but he kept auditioning for acting roles. He eventually became one of the most famous leading men of film, produced his own movies, and remains a cultural icon.

- **Manoj Bhargava**—A tax driver until thirty years of age, he pursued his dreams, becoming a billionaire entrepreneur and founder of 5-hour Energy, the successful beverage company.

- **J. K. Rowling**—As a single mom on welfare at age thirty-one, she stuck to her vision of becoming an author and today is best known as the author of the best-selling Harry Potter books.

- **Ray Kroc**—After working as a salesperson of paper cups and milkshake mixers, he purchased McDonald's and turned it into the most successful fast-food chain in the world.

The stories may be different, but the common thread among all these people is that they didn't choose a conventional path to success. They kept on pushing, despite the odds. So next time you meet someone successful, don't just look at how much money or success they have. Focus on what got them to success. Warriors know how to rise above their circumstances or situations.

Failure is not just an opportunity to learn but also a chance to reincarnate. With the right mindset, you can go back, try something different, and emerge transformed. A warrior must be able to build on the premise that the next time is going to be better when they decide to do something differently. Doing the same thing repeatedly will not yield better results.

FAILURE IS NOT JUST AN OPPORTUNITY TO LEARN BUT ALSO A CHANCE FOR REINCARNATION.

Even a little hope is better than hopelessness. Hope has much to do with a strong mental and emotional mindset. We don't often talk about hope in the business world, but it's important. Hope can inspire positive action, bringing us to a new state where we can do things differently, better than we did in the past. A warrior must be able to review and assess what has happened, what's really going on and what to do, but their hope can inspire them forward. It can give them a perspective on what happened in the past. They can recognize it and learn from a past event but not dwell on it because it's behind them, and they have the hope of a better future, something they can build toward.

That said, just hoping will not solve your dilemma. You can hope forever, but you still need to act. This is where your action plan comes into play. You're learning, so now devise your plan for delivering yourself from this situation, innovating and making it brand-new.

FOLLOW THROUGH

There is no one key to overcoming setbacks and failure. It is a combination of many small and significant efforts on your part. When you have come so far, going through rigorous preparation and training, empowering yourself to win on all fronts, gaining control over your decisions and actions, developing your skills, and poising yourself to take action, you have paved the way for physical and mental toughness. Find your strength in this, the courage to keep going. Even if you must write a new chapter in this season or build from an earlier point, proceed. Follow through. You are focused, you are mentally present, you know what your mission is, and you won't quit now when you have held yourself accountable and taken ownership. It is time for you to lead yourself and lead others out of the situation.

Follow-through is especially important because you don't want to start something and not see it to the end or execute it adequately. Following through makes an incredible difference in the quality of the outcome. You must do the follow-through at the right time with the right people. And we believe that awareness and attentiveness can lead us in finding the right people at that time.

This reminds us of a great quote from Tao Te Ching: "When the student is ready, the teacher will appear. When the student is truly ready, the teacher will disappear."

Following through is what puts you back into the action. When you take action, you'll be more disinclined to give up. Following through puts you in touch with everything around you and gives you the awareness you need. Everyone is excited when something is just getting started, but often people become distracted by other priorities or lose their enthusiasm somewhere along the way. This is when so many companies, projects, and people don't succeed, when they fail to follow through. What happens then is that people reach the stage where they realize things aren't working. They wonder if they should quit. But you must ask yourself the following: Did I do what I had to do? Was I committed? Did I hold myself accountable for seeing things through?

When you take responsibility and are accountable, following through is part of the process, and it becomes second nature. It is part of communication, sometimes to yourself. Not following through leaves your teams out of touch with your goals and the steps needed to get there, and they may not know the stage or progress of a particular project. They will lack awareness of the situation, which will limit their ability to contribute to it. You could lose the engagement of team members, fall behind with milestones, compromise the quality of your products or services, jeopardize your relationships or reputation, and probably lose out on opportunities as a result. The worst-case scenario is that all previous efforts didn't lead anywhere or amount to much—so not following through comes at a great cost. You can't make time run in reverse, and you can't alter or bring back what's in the past.

Build follow-through into your everyday business practice systems. When follow-through becomes part of your daily routine and method of operation, it becomes a highly effective way to build resilience, stay focused, and achieve your goals. Invest your time and efforts into attentively addressing and listening to the needs of your clients, colleagues, partners, and community. We regularly stay in touch with clients and external environments. This keeps us informed, on top of things, connected, and better aware of pain points so we can address critical issues in a timely manner.

If you're consistently following through, you will see good, long-term results. In following through, you also discover lots of important things and gain key insights. You might realize you need to change direction, for example. You learn how to better face situations and pivot and adapt as needed. It's about being attentive, demonstrating your commitment, and taking the time to invest in your clients, employees, and supplier partners.

KNOW HOW TO CALCULATE LOSSES WHILE STILL MOVING FORWARD

As all warriors do, you will suffer losses. This is part of entering and fighting in the battle for the greater cause. But a warrior in business must be able to take the losses while still proceeding into battle. When you've experienced losses, assess the situation, taking stock of what's gone or what has been compromised before you determine the action forward.

YOU HAVE THE ABILITY TO REVERSE YOUR FAILURES.

Calculating losses in war or business is not just a numbers game. It involves taking an inventory of the whole situation and assessing individual components but also thinking more widely about where you are, where you need to be, and where you might end up. Don't lose heart in the face of losses, and don't consider them failures. Losses happen. If you focus only on what you've lost, then you've taken your eyes off where you could go and what you still stand to gain. Your losses could intensify if you don't take action to regroup, reinvest, and redo. You have the ability to reverse your failures.

In real-life situations, when you look at any project and realize it's not going well, you may experience disillusionment, be tempted to change things midstream, or even consider quitting. At that moment, you must take action to change the outcome. Even if you have calculated potential losses during your preparation stage, things still may not go your way, and you may end up losing more than you'd anticipated. Remember that hesitation breeds inaction. Without deliberate action on your part, those uncontrollable forces may hold you down longer than you envisioned, and being knocked down so hard can lead to paralysis and further inaction. That is why it's crucial to get up, dust yourself off, and get moving as soon as possible. Don't let the ugly thought of quitting consume your thoughts for even a second. Throw it away immediately. Continue marching forward, even if you have the slightest inkling that you can't do it. The moment you feel those doubts is the moment you most need to regroup and streamline your thoughts, gathering every bit of courage in you to stick your neck out and keep moving. You have all the skills and the knowledge you need to turn your situation around. You have the ability to proceed with calmness and mental strength, courage, and conviction.

RESILIENCE IS NOT JUST ABOUT BOUNCING BACK BUT BOUNCING FORWARD.

Dan Gable, Olympic gold medalist and renowned wrestling coach, once said, "Gold medals aren't really made of gold. They're made of sweat, determination, and a hard-to-find alloy called guts." A warrior in business must have the guts to go for the gold. Remember and reflect on what we've talked about up to this point and use it to reframe your mental state, strengthen your resolve, and push yourself to victory in battle. Keep fighting!

Resilience is not just about bouncing back but bouncing forward. The warrior in business never quits. They get back up immediately after being knocked down, knowing that any hesitation is an opportunity for self-doubt to take hold and prevent them from taking the next necessary action to achieve their goal. They know that on the journey to success, they'll have setbacks and disappointments, but they look for a way to overcome these, to turn their failures into lessons to fuel further progress, recognizing that their resilience is dependent on this mindset. The ability to stick to your goals and objectives, never losing sight of your original vision, is a crucial skill you can learn to cultivate with practice, the right training, and self-discipline. If you allow your driving purpose to loom larger in your mind than any obstacle you could ever face, then you will lose your fear of failure and commit instead to seeing your plans through with the knowledge that every challenge you overcome today will only increase your resiliency tomorrow.

Executive Summary

- The adversity you will face **will knock you down permanently if you let it**.

- Resilience requires **courage, grit, creativity, and the determination to succeed**.

- Your **mindset can help you take on the challenges you face**, turn them into something positive and transformative, and keep going.

- Failure can be **a stepping stone to learning**.

- **Your own will** can pull you out of any circumstances.

- In business, you're going to succeed or fail—but **with the right mindset, you win either way**.

- If you **consistently follow through**, you will see good, long-term results.

- Hesitation breeds inaction. The moment you are knocked down, **gather your courage, and make the choice to push ahead**.

- Resilience is not just about bouncing back but **bouncing forward**.

CHAPTER 7

A WARRIOR IN BUSINESS FIGHTS THE GOOD FIGHT

―――――――――――――――――――

A WARRIOR IN BUSINESS ISN'T JUST TASKED with fighting to achieve success; they're also charged with fighting the *good* fight. This means something greater in the big scheme of things. The good fight is more than money, reputation, or influence. It's not just about having a steady stream of clients or people who seek them out. It goes beyond winning awards and being at the forefront of their industry. In everything they do, a warrior in business is concerned about people's welfare. They're clear on what they're fighting for and defend a cause, something that has meaning and value. They're just and fair in their approach, operating with integrity and protecting what needs to be protected, and each day they are on a mission to make a positive impact. Their work and its effects are their legacy.

When you fight the absolute best fight in your daily work, you become more analytical about what you do. You establish a mindset that informs the way you approach everyday decisions—decisions that are made with the heart. You wish the best for those around you, elevate others, and are generous with your gifts and skills. The principles behind fighting the good fight should be part of your core business operating principles. They anchor your success to things that are lasting. Resilience takes on a different meaning when you work like this. Challenges, crises, projects, initiatives . . . you think about them differently when you approach them with a mindset that rises above the materialistic achievements.

Fighting the good fight means trying your hardest to be the best version of yourself every day. You manage life's battles with a deeper strength and generosity of spirit. But this is hard, and you will not be effective at it unless you have the right mindset and process behind it. You must learn how to shape yourself personally in this way and then proceed forward with a service attitude toward your thoughts and actions. You're not just working for yourself; you're also working for others and doing it for the greater good.

BRING OUT THE BEST IN OTHERS

Fighting the good fight has everything to do with other people. There's a famous proverb from the Bible that's referenced in business quite frequently. It says, "As iron sharpens iron, so one person sharpens another" (Proverbs 27:17, NIV). As a warrior in business, you should have a mindset focused on lifting others up and helping them reach their fullest potential through your interactions with them. Iron sharpening iron means no one is alone; instead, they rely on one another to make each other better. You need to have people involved in your ventures who not only help make you better, but whom you can help make better too. This is possible if we are mindful of the way we engage, motivate, challenge, and inspire one another. In your business, you are responsible for your people, and they are responsible for what you've tasked them with. You need one another to grow and achieve your company's mission.

YOU NEED ONE ANOTHER TO GROW AND ACHIEVE YOUR COMPANY'S MISSION.

In an organization like this, people care for one another, their clients, and the community, no matter what capacity they serve in. From the higher-ups to those in the supporting roles, from internal team members to external suppliers, the idea is to work in the best interests of others. Let's face it, without all of them, there would be no business. A warrior in business needs to be willing to do the right things for the people who make their business possible.

Be Willing to Be Shaped Personally

Before you can "sharpen" others with what you do, we should take a close look at ourselves. Fighting the good fight is really about leadership. You can't lead others unless you know how to lead yourself first. The kind of success that matters in the long run starts with your mindset as a leader first. When you work on yourself and align yourself with what's important, you will develop the traits of a warrior in business and allow these traits to inform your actions, which will transform the way you work and how you interact with others.

YOU CAN'T LEAD OTHERS UNLESS YOU KNOW HOW TO LEAD YOURSELF FIRST.

Small and midsize business owners work especially hard to achieve success, pushing toward a profitable outcome and investing a great deal of themselves. Particularly in smaller businesses, the stakes are very high. Fighting the good fight is what allows a business warrior to choose their battles wisely and apply all their preparation, training, and expertise to what matters. And that ability will improve resilience for their business, their team, and themselves exponentially. Never forget that resiliency as a team starts with you as the leader. It is your resilience that will bring about success, driving meaningful engagement not just at work but also in every other facet of your life. You want to ensure that the energy you devote to your business will make a difference in the long term, and you want to work in a way that's meaningful and fulfilling, allowing you to build the kind of legacy that's worth leaving.

Learning how to be the kind of leader who fights the good fight involves not just your IQ (intelligence quotient) but also your EQ (emotional quotient) and SQ (spiritual quotient). There are tangible things we can do to improve our leadership IQ, including training. But more and more, EQ and SQ are areas where a leader must excel if they genuinely want to be effective in business. Raising your spiritual quotient doesn't require you to be religious, but rather, it demands that you look deeply inside yourself to understand who you are on a spiritual level. It is a lengthy process to develop in any of these areas, and it requires careful self-examination and perhaps the guidance of a good coach or mentor. You need EQ and SQ to be stable; without them, IQ doesn't mean a darn thing. All three pieces come together as part of your leadership capacity. A leader needs to think about all the parts that make up who they are. Be intentional about building up and fostering the important parts of yourself so that you have the maximum to give. This is what it means to lead yourself.

Leadership is often misunderstood. It isn't about position, power, or money. Those are all ego drivers, and you need to recognize them for what they are if you're going to become a warrior in business. Leadership is about how you lead yourself and your people every day toward your mission and goals. It informs what you do and how you do it on a day-to-day basis. Your responsibility is to build an environment where your people thrive. But before you can do that, you must ensure that you can help yourself thrive first. Your willingness, acceptance, and desire to change yourself for the better is fundamental. Credentials will only get you so far. When you focus on your capacity rather than your capabilities, you can think critically, innovate, adapt, and collaborate, becoming more resilient in the process. After ensuring that you are able to lead yourself, to grow your capacity for success and leadership, to raise your IQ, EQ, and SQ—then you can turn your gaze outward and think about who you're operating for.

FOCUS ON YOUR CAPACITY RATHER THAN YOUR CAPABILITIES.

At the end of the day, when you've given it your all, you want to be able to say you fought the good fight and did your absolute best. Fighting the good fight is what makes you resilient. It's what gives you the ability to work with intention on the important, lasting things, contributing meaningfully to your business, your spheres of influence, your community, and the world. People often measure success by how much money they've earned. But when you do the right thing, success follows. And yes, that often means money too.

Choose the People in Your Inner Circle

The people you choose to have around you make a difference. Just like you sharpen them with your leadership, they sharpen you with their different gifts, abilities, and perspectives. It's easy in business to build a sort of wall around yourself, especially if, as a leader, you feel you can't let people see that you have vulnerabilities. But to grow and take your business to the next level, you have to accept that you need the help of others. Their perceptions, sensibilities, knowledge, and experience collectively make your business stronger and better. Don't be hesitant to be real with them. Allow for transparency in your work life and align yourself with people who see the real you. If you wish to succeed in business, you will need to seek guidance and advice from them at critical moments.

The people around you have a vested interest in you and the well-being of your company. Like you, they want to see your business succeed and feel that their efforts and contributions toward building it were well spent. Foster an environment where iron sharpens iron, where your employees are not afraid to talk to you. This means you must allow them—even encourage them—to ask you questions or even confront you when something seems amiss to them. You can't be the best version of yourself if people only tell you what you want to hear.

Be a mentor to those around you but allow them to mentor you as well. A good leader is open to learning and willing to be coached. Since you can't always do this with your employees, invite people from elsewhere in your industry, allowing for a peer-group dynamic where you can receive coaching and advice. The goal is to always improve on what you do and how you do it in the best interests of others. Everyone, no matter how long we've been doing business, can use the advice and objective opinions of others.

KNOW WHAT YOUR PURPOSE IS

What wakes you up in the morning? What's your purpose for getting out of bed? Having a clear understanding of the meaning and goals that drive your work will enable you to fight the good fight. Finding your purpose gives you a deeper understanding of who you are as a person and a more complete understanding of why you exist and how you can help others. Having a purpose will help you define a set of core values to guide your business decisions. Your own business is ideally a vehicle for you to apply your passions and talents to something the world needs. It's a bonus that you can make a profit and contribute to larger economic development in the process. Defining the purpose of your business makes you more resilient when external and internal situations change drastically. Businesses founded around a clear purpose tend to work with focus and effectiveness. They have an easier time rallying people behind their work. And identifying and communicating their message is easy, allowing them to build strong reputations and brand loyalty within their spaces.

We've always believed that the purpose behind our own business, S&A Consulting Group, is that our work should be a win-win for all—something that's sustainable for everyone. That has been the hallmark of our every undertaking and initiative since the company's inception. If we had not considered ourselves warriors in business who fought the good fight, then we would not have made it this far. The difference we are making in the lives of people may be small in comparison to some organizations, but the principles, thought process, and heart we bring to helping and empowering others guide us daily. Every morning when we wake up, we think and ask ourselves how we can make a difference that day. As entrepreneurs and leaders, we know we have a responsibility to carry out our mission of improving conditions for others. We see each of our clients and partners as an individual, so we customize our approach for them to ensure we're meeting each of their needs in the way that best serves them. This aspect of our business is what creates meaning and value for us.

SUCCESS ENTAILS FAR MORE THAN JUST THE MERE ACCUMULATION OF WEALTH OR ACHIEVEMENT OF STATUS.

Yes, you're definitely in business to make money, to establish your reputation, and to put yourself in a good position. But a warrior in business does not only concern themselves with the typical drivers as dictated by the world but also recognizes that success entails far more than the mere accumulation of wealth or achievement of status. The warrior seeks to find a feeling of abundance. This helps them to work harder and more sustainably, allowing them to remain positive and hopeful in tough times. Seeking abundance has the additional benefit of bearing out the aphorism that if you cultivate good, it will come back to you. Working the law of reciprocity into your everyday life builds better business relationships. If you are good to other people, they will be good to you in return.

FOCUS ON THE WELL-BEING OF OTHERS

A warrior in business knows what they're fighting for and fiercely defends their cause. Fighting the good fight implies that there's something important, something good worth fighting for. It's a call to action. A warrior who fights the good fight remains anchored in their cause. They don't lose sight of what's important. They work tirelessly, continuously fighting, even when it feels like they have nothing left.

You have a responsibility to your business, but you also have a civic responsibility. As a leader, your concern for others and the action you take to improve their lives is fundamental to the integrity of your business. You must be devoted to the cause of your business but also willing to work toward causes outside of it. It's great to do things within the framework of your business, but a warrior goes above and beyond their everyday boundaries, expending their efforts to give in other areas of need. To cultivate this mindset, look for opportunities that allow you to contribute and add to the world around you. Remember that being resilient means you're always looking at the bigger picture. You should also focus on the needs of others and seek out solutions to their problems without being asked. In this way, you can help yourself and build up your business by lifting others up.

As business warriors, we've intentionally looked for ways to help others, including recognizing and collaborating with other men and women who are fighting the good fight in their own spaces. We seek to be inspired by them while we seek to inspire others by modeling what we believe and showing that what we say is important to us. We believe that as warriors, we must give back something socially viable to our community. The community supports us, and in turn, we support it.

One of our philanthropic efforts was our 2005 establishment of the Elite Women Around the World (EWAW) Foundation, a nonprofit that honors and empowers women and organizations working tirelessly to shape and build their communities. EWAW is a global network of individuals, leaders, organizations, and businesses who come together with a shared mission to develop, grow, and support the economic and social stability of women and girls through entrepreneurial and leadership programs. In our work through this organization, we've been thrilled to recognize many people over the past several years with the Global ALPHA Woman Award and various other leadership awards. These inspirational leaders are from diverse industries, age groups, socioeconomic statuses, and ethnicities. We are proud of our work for this organization's positive impact on so many lives.

Exercise: Where Is Your Effort Most Needed?

Consider what's important to *you*. There are many causes you could devote your energy to outside of business, but it is essential that the cause you choose reflects your purpose and aligns with who you are on an emotional and spiritual level. As a warrior in business, devote yourself to whatever cause speaks to your soul. Those causes are life-giving and important, and they will enrich what you do. To explore where your efforts are most needed, answer these questions for yourself:

- Who do I want to lift up and support?
- What causes do I want to defend?
- What problems in the world need to be solved?
- When did I most need help in my life? Who is in that position now?
- Where, or to whom, is my unique individual skill set most useful?
- How do I want to be remembered?

Once you understand your unique purpose, you can shape your work around that. Your work should be focused on answering the question, How best can we serve? A warrior doesn't need the promise of results or recognition to fight the good fight. Rather than needing to get something out of it, they simply look for what they can *do*. People with a servant-leader mindset develop strong bonds and relationships with other people, which elevates the work they do. If you focus on what is best for the people you serve, then the organizational and personal rewards will take care of themselves. You will ultimately have more success and opportunities because *people*—not money, power, or position—are your top priority and focus. In adopting this mindset, you have the power to create a snowball effect on culture, climate, and productivity—improving things for everyone.

BUILD POSITIVE SOCIAL RELATIONSHIPS

Resiliency doesn't simply mean focusing on your own personal strengths and overcoming the odds. Positive social relationships are one of the essential keys to resilience. Creating and building stronger social connections increases the resiliency of human beings, and the same is true for businesses as well. Relationships are connections you can draw strength from when needed to help overcome adversity.

Building relationships should be an ongoing effort. Think of ways you can nurture and deepen your relationship. It does not happen overnight. Each relationship must be carefully tended and nurtured before you can reap its rewards.

We have taken great care to build lasting business relationships. When we started out back in 1989, we had no clients, few friends, and no money. It was very lonely. But both of us thought that the best way to grow our business was to get involved and start serving in various professional and civic organizations. Rita started volunteering and actively participated in various organizations, such as the Council of Smaller Enterprises (COSE), Urban League, Small Business Administration (SBA), Federation of India Community Association, chambers of commerce, financial institutions, and so on. Nip gave back to his industry in a positive way by serving on various committees of the Investment Casting Institute, which he has been continuously involved with since 1991. He has helped many young interns and other fellow members, educating and mentoring them on how to lead in the industry.

We gave our time and talents and served the small-business community generously, assisting with financial management, business planning, access to capital, and development of entrepreneurial and leadership skills. Some of these same people came back to us to become our clients. Many of them have remained our clients for the past thirty-plus years. As a result, we feel we have established an emotional connection with the community. Through our relationships and involvement, we were able to not only find great talent for our organization but also solve many of our clients' problems by connecting them to resources they would not have had access to without our network.

LEADERSHIP IS A WAY OF LIFE FOR US.

Through these powerful resources, alliances, partnerships, collaborations, and collective experiences of dealing with situations out of our control, we were able to get through many hardships, which we could not have faced alone. Our resiliency today is due to the strong and genuine relationships we invested our time and talent in. Leadership is a way of life for us. Living leadership every day and making sure that we continue to give back to the community where we work and live is important.

The operating principle of our organization is that we serve people and live humbly. Through the power of these relationships, we became not only subject-matter experts in our areas but also a trusted resource for other businesses, both with respect to improving their products and services and how to best serve their people. Our purpose is not to seek recognition but to create meaning and add value to those around us. We are proud to share that in our effort to fight the good fight, we have received numerous testimonials and awards on local, regional, and global levels for making a difference in people's lives.

BE JUST AND FAIR

As business owners, we not only believe but also exemplify in our daily practices that all people are equal, have a shared common humanity, and have a right to realize their full potential as individuals, families, and communities. These days, people often talk about equity, inclusion, and diversity. It has become a prime topic of concern for most organizations of any size. Equity doesn't mean *equal*, however. As defined by the Marin County Department of Health and Human Services, "Equality means each individual or group of people is given the same resources or opportunities. Equity recognizes that each person has different circumstances and allocates the exact resources and opportunities needed to reach an equitable outcome."[5]

FIGHTING THE GOOD FIGHT IS HARD. YOU WILL NEED A FIRM GRIP ON YOUR IDEALS.

Warriors in business abide by rules that are ethical and fair. Fairness is the key. Everyone should receive the same opportunities, no matter where they come from, what they look like, or what their background is. Fairness means you're impartial and treat others justly, without favoritism or bias. Warriors in business do the right thing by seeking to make good choices and trying to get others to do the same. They pursue a good outcome. But fighting the good fight is hard. You will need a firm grip on your ideals.

ACT WITH INTEGRITY

Working with integrity means that you live and operate in truth and stand behind principles that are in the best interests of others. When you have integrity, you are transparent and accepting of that responsibility. It takes discipline and character to fight gracefully and uphold your ideals. To have integrity is a real responsibility to yourself, your people, your organization, and the community.

Integrity establishes trust. That's especially important in business. Your

---

5 "Equity vs. Equality: What's the Difference?" Marin County, Department of Health and Human Services, April 2021, https://www.marinhhs.org/sites/default/files/boards/general/equality_v._equity_04_05_2021.pdf.

clients and workforce should know they can trust in and rely on you. With integrity, you earn the respect of others without asking for it. The simplest way to understand and practice integrity in business is to think about it as a noble profession, where values and morals are important. Integrity is having the ability to set aside your differences and behave honorably and ethically, holding yourself to a higher standard and trying to get others to do so as well. This mindset conveys the value you bring as a human being and a leader. If you establish that you care for others and will always be a watchdog for them, you will have longevity in your relationships and business. Leaders with integrity understand that their actions, words, and decisions shape the company's values, culture, and morale. They value their customers, become role models for their teams, and act with good intentions rather than with selfish motives.

PROTECT THOSE IN NEED

Warriors go beyond themselves to protect and take care of the well-being of others for the greater good. From our vantage point, we believe there must be more business warriors standing up for others in companies, boardrooms, and in the community. We have too few leaders who are willing to use their influence to defend those in need.

Even if you are not a corporate leader, you may have the opportunity to step up in other ways. Perhaps it will be taking a stand against deceptive practices in the company where you work, speaking out against sexual harassment, or talking with your coworker if they act in an inappropriate manner with a fellow employee.

It takes courage to step out and push back against injustice. It will mean that you don't go with the flow. Sometimes, standing firm to give voice to what you feel is right means standing alone. But it's not just about the processes, procedures, structures, or systems. *People* make up organizations. And it's people who will see you lifting your voice to aid what is good and righteous. Those who do good must assume the responsibility of warriors—to *protect*.

It's the human beings who work alongside you, who help you achieve your goals and mission, who must be protected. People working in your organization are the most important assets you have, and taking care of those people and preserving the trust and depth of your relationships with them should be among your highest priorities. When you care for these relationships, you are not only investing in the well-being of your organization today but also ensuring its resilience in the future. By fighting the good fight each and every day, you will cultivate the mindset of a business warrior—first, to lead yourself, then to lead your people, and always to serve your community. In this way, your success as a leader will be defined not by your earning potential but by your capacity to lead others and help them thrive. If you are successful in that much more strenuous and rewarding endeavor, monetary gain and professional recognition will follow.

Executive Summary

- Fighting the good fight means **trying your hardest to be the best version of yourself.**

- The kind of leader who fights the good fight possesses not just **IQ (intelligence quotient),** but also **EQ (emotional quotient) and SQ (spiritual quotient).**

- Your willingness, acceptance, and desire to **change yourself for the better** is essential if you are to be an effective leader.

- **Invite honesty from those you lead**; you can't be the best version of yourself if people only tell you what you want to hear.

- Having a purpose will help you **define a set of core values to guide your business decisions.**

- A warrior doesn't need **the promise of results or recognition** to fight the good fight.

- **The relationships you build** with your workforce, clients, and community over time will make or break your business.

- Warriors in business **abide by rules that are ethical and fair.** They are impartial and treat others justly, without favoritism or bias.

- To have integrity is **a real responsibility to yourself, your people, your organization, and the community**.

- Good leaders are willing to **use their influence to defend those in need**.

CHAPTER 8

A WARRIOR IN BUSINESS ENGAGES, ACTIVATES, AND INSPIRES OTHERS

THE FOUNDATION OF HOW YOU ENGAGE, ACTIVATE, and inspire others is built on two things: your relationships with people and how you communicate with them. A warrior in business is courageous enough to fight alone if needed, but they also never lose sight of their teammates, employees, clients, or the competition. They enjoy seeing others win and cheering them on. They engage with others in a way that preserves and supports their relationships. They are dependable and trustworthy themselves and work to develop trusting relationships with others. They bring together teams that understand loyalty and are protective. They act as builders. They empower their people to think creatively and innovate. They reward those who have the courage of creativity, not just material success. They are not worried about financial outcomes alone and are focused on the human side of business: cultivating and winning the hearts, minds, and dedication of their people. The business warrior is an inclusive leader, taking care to build up women and minority leaders.

Nothing happens in a vacuum, so when you engage with others intentionally, you develop people, build a positive and productive work culture, and encourage the right way to lead. Intentionality is making a conscious effort, not presuming something will happen by itself. You are proactive about taking the first step. You make sure you take the initiative and follow up. The bottom line is to empower your people.

For most of us, simply having a job isn't enough—we need to feel connected to a bigger purpose, whether through carrying out our organization's mission or our own development. That's why understanding how to engage, activate, and inspire your team is necessary for success. It is necessary if you want your people to be prepared to overcome challenges and adversity to become a resilient workforce.

We're never alone in business. We will always have employees, customers, and supplier partners. Unless you foster good relationships, you won't succeed. That's life. And life's principles apply to business; whether you have a one-person operation or a thousand-person company, the same principles apply. You've got to learn first to work with others, help them to develop, trust them, and engage them. The same holds true for customers.

WE'RE NEVER ALONE IN BUSINESS.

The specific nature of each of your relationships is critical. Your relationship dynamic may be different with employees, customers, clients, vendors, supplier partners, coworkers, people in your industry, mentors, and external stakeholders. You need to be attuned to the different business relationships so you will be able to meet their needs. It's about building the bridge through connections and trust and about showing you're invested in others. When you invest in engaging and inspiring your team, you create a culture where everyone can flourish, and your business can achieve significant success.

There are immense benefits when you activate, engage, and inspire others. These include

- Gaining opportunities
- Achieving business growth
- Advancing goals
- Gaining insights that are good for your business
- Creating alliances
- Building a reputation
- Increasing resources you can lean on
- Gaining new perspectives
- Seeing how well you're serving others

FOSTER GOOD RELATIONSHIPS

A warrior in business interacts with others in a way that maintains strong and supportive relationships. For them, relationship-building is a two-way street. You give and you receive. A business warrior uses several ways to inspire and bring out the best in others.

They value helping people live to their fullest potential and are intentional about offering value to others. They are generous in sharing their knowledge and resources and going the extra mile. They make themselves available by regularly checking in, expressing gratitude, and welcoming feedback.

In our own business, we believe in building and nurturing relationships. We can't be effective in what we do if we don't walk the talk. Over the years, we've been continually making an intentional effort and have firsthand experience in building relationships with our clients, employees, supplier partners, and community in our hometown of Cleveland. We extended this in the work we did with other clients in the USA and around the world. Many times, we went out of our way because we recognized the importance of personally meeting and staying connected with people. This is one of the reasons we've been able to maintain our current client relationships for an extended period of time.

A warrior in business is dependable, trustworthy, and follows through. Nip talks with many people, but he makes sure to follow up with personal calls, emails, and various other ways. He's intentional about following through, and whether it culminates in a business proposition for mutual gain is not the ultimate goal. We both see the value in building, supporting, and maintaining good relationships.

When you are leading, transparency in business is necessary. Transparency creates open communication, not only building trust among your team but also helping to make you more approachable. People will feel more comfortable speaking with you. That is how you earn their trust, and at the same time, it will create a foundation for a healthy relationship. If you want your organization to grow and be sustainable and successful, you must find ways to engage people and make them attentive to your company's goals.

But what does transparency really mean? It means disclosing the deserved information to your people and being truthful about it. It means sharing both good and bad information. When you and your team work together toward a shared goal, your people need to have clear direction and openness on the why and the how. Many times, this conversation will be extremely uncomfortable and tough, but it must be communicated to your people, which will help the organization to move forward. Tackle the tough conversation in such a way that it helps the other person better understand your purpose and to believe why this change is necessary. This may even improve the situation or relationship.

Why is transparency important? We've seen the way it fosters a workplace culture of open communication and accountable behavior. Everyone clearly understands their responsibilities and level of authority in your team. As a business warrior, when you maintain transparency, you are creating unity and trust among your people and building a resilient workforce.

It is your communication that will take a starring role in activating, engaging, and inspiring those around you. Simultaneously, this happens on two levels:

- **On a personal level**, a warrior in business communicates intentionally, using language that is uniquely meaningful to the individual, rather than relying on business jargon. You must communicate openly and respectfully, using inclusive language. This shows your empathy—that you care for people and their feelings. It also shows interest in their lives. Business warriors are considerate, compassionate, concerned, and thoughtful, which is what sets them apart. They see the human being first and communicate with them in a way that resonates.

- **On an organizational level**, the warrior in business builds people up. They know how to empower people. They practice purpose-driven leadership with people skills and translate their purpose into action. Your actions must be rooted in your interest in other people's lives, so others feel valued. When people feel valued, they develop a state of mind that makes them willing to go above and beyond in their performance. People will actually enjoy coming to work because they feel inspired and engaged and do meaningful work. This will directly impact your business's success and profitability.

The business warrior not only finds their own purpose but helps others find their purpose as well. This fosters unity around your vision, mission, and goals. To do this, you will need to become a storyteller, someone who knows how to interpret and weave the facts and data, possesses insight, and effectively communicates at all levels of the organization. You have to be a good storyteller to help people connect and "see and feel" themselves in what you're sharing. You're not just talking about business; you're also connecting with the emotional side of people. The baseline of this is how effectively you communicate. The message you deliver must contain facts and data, but if you convey it in an engaging, meaningful, and relevant way, your message will be much more effective. When you help others arrive at necessary insights, you help them to connect the dots, and you use the information to move them toward action.

INTENTIONALLY BUILD A COMPETENT WORK CULTURE

A competent work culture should look like a blend of shared beliefs and values. Wherever you seek to value the unique identities and contributions of all people, you must respect the differences of others, have faith and trust in one another, learn from each other, communicate across cultures effectively, and educate each other about the proper ways to think, act, and feel. In a competent work culture, you will become mindful of the diverse needs of the employees, partners, communities, and consumers you serve. This way, people will flourish and become resilient, prepared to face any challenges.

PEOPLE WILL FLOURISH AND BECOME RESILIENT, PREPARED TO FACE ANY CHALLENGES.

As mentioned throughout the book, a warrior in business is intentional in building relationships with employees, peers, partners, and other stakeholders, creating a social connection. The corporate culture should impact the employee experience. When you serve as a leader, coach, or entrepreneur, irrespective of your role in an organization, you need to be sure that you are building a resilient culture that fosters resilient people. The culture of your business is your company's identity.

When disruption occurs, employees are often left dealing with feelings of fear and uncertainty that impact their engagement, productivity, and service levels. If you foster a culture that values resilience, by supporting activities that embrace change, you have lit the spark to propel your organization forward. Building a thriving team requires a keen sense of self-awareness, cultural intelligence, listening skills, and empathy. The warrior in business continually and consistently thinks, develops, and facilitates growth and self-development and leads others to become great. Again, a business warrior is not hesitant for themselves or their people to receive coaching, guidance, mentoring, and consulting when it comes to personal and professional growth and development.

A competent work culture

- Fosters teamwork and collaboration

- Builds community

- Increases engagement

- Creates more job satisfaction

- Attracts and retains talent

- Improves performance

- Is known for its good business reputation

- Maintains people's commitment

What's relevant for one business isn't applicable to all. But how you interact with others and what you practice every day in your business dealings is critical. To succeed, compete, and collaborate in today's interconnected world, understanding and working with diverse cultures is of the utmost importance. It is no longer a choice. When we create a culture centered on shared values and goals, people feel activated, engaged, and inspired to do meaningful work.

IT TAKES TIME AND COMMITMENT TO EDUCATE YOURSELF.

Cultural competence has helped us build long-standing relationships and grow our business in the USA and around the globe. With clients in various countries, it was vital for us to be able to communicate and collaborate effectively. Building relationships and working successfully with people from different countries and cultures no doubt present some major challenges. It takes time and commitment to educate yourself. Over the years, we have consistently made an up-front effort to collaborate effectively with customers, clients, and businesses from different countries and cultures, learning their languages and cultural etiquettes, their social likes, and their dislikes. This process requires both commitment and investment. We make sure that our people communicate and interact effectively with people who have varying beliefs and schedules. In addition, we stay informed about global issues so we can guide and inform our clients of industry trends that may impact them positively or negatively. Working with our overseas clients, we listen attentively, use clear, concise sentences, and avoid using slang. We generally follow up verbal communication with an email to ease the minds of our clients. This helps to prevent mistakes and misunderstandings. We treat every conversation as a learning opportunity.

As the business grew, we became more tolerant of clients' beliefs, faiths, customs, values, traditions, and behaviors. It has become the way we think and continues to be an ongoing process. We appreciate being able to interact with people of diverse cultures, not only to build respect but also to learn from various personalities and societies. It provides us with a holistic approach to the way we do business in our local community and around the world.

At one point, Nip was chosen to be a consultant to a Japanese conglomerate. He asked the selection committee why, out of the many consultants they'd interviewed, they had selected him. Their answer was that they thought he would bring "the best blend of East and West."

Our interactions with different people from many cultures have resulted in a great unity of thoughts and shared ideas. As a result, we have learned how to appreciate and learn from the various perspectives and views of others. This experience has definitely strengthened our relationships with our clients, improved our customer service, and become part of our everyday work-life culture.

EMPOWER YOUR PEOPLE TOWARD CREATIVE THINKING AND INNOVATION

A warrior in business invites creativity, innovation, and fresh solutions. They know that when they put their heads together with others, the ideas are better and include a greater diversity of perspectives, opinions, and experiences than if they had been working alone. Creativity and innovation allow you to adapt and change more easily. They enable your business to overcome challenges, they promote growth, and they can increase your productivity.

Innovation is an exciting way to pull people out of their comfort zones and invite them into a new space. By inviting others to innovate, you give them an opportunity to show up and think outside the box, brainstorm new ideas, and go the extra mile to come up with unique solutions.

Giants like Amazon, Google, Apple, and Pixar have effectively inspired innovation in their organizations. They have their own strategies to encourage inspiration. Google is known for its culture of innovation, where employees are encouraged to spend 20 percent of their time working on side projects that may not necessarily be related to their main job. This has led to the creation of many successful products, including Google Maps and Gmail.

Small-to-midsize businesses can also take steps to help their teams reach their full innovative potential. Fostering a culture of innovation in your organization is the key. Have an open communication policy where everyone can share their ideas and not be afraid to fail. Empower your leaders who can empower their people with the freedom to think. Give them encouragement, tools, support, and resources to experiment with innovative ideas. This encourages your people to work with entrepreneurial spirit, so they have the courage to take risks.

When we moved to the office location before our current location, our space was built with an open layout (with the exception of the executive offices), which encouraged people to collaborate and interact freely. We held weekly brainstorming sessions to think of new ways of serving our clients. Over the years, we routinely rewarded our people, including our supplier partners, with recognition awards and consistently showed our appreciation for their efforts.

Warriors in business focus on strengths rather than weaknesses. They reward people for creative thinking, not just success. The warrior in business welcomes the sharing of innovative ideas, recognizing that these might give birth to something new. They understand that as part of the process, failure is acceptable and viewed as a lesson learned. This gives their people room to grow, try, practice, and explore. Creative thinking and innovation don't usually happen when you're doing your routine work. They come when you have the freedom to explore without fear of failure or repercussions. They come when you are engaged and encouraged to explore innovative ideas and work in a culture that inspires change.

BE LOYAL TO AND PROTECTIVE OF YOUR PEOPLE

Warriors are loyal to their people and organization, standing up for them and the company's mission. They take their responsibility to protect others seriously, and they keep working and showing up with the intention to make their environment and the world a better place.

They speak their truth and are comfortable standing up for what they believe is right. They are loyal to the cause and never lose sight of it. Warriors can be fierce yet compassionate, gentle, and caring, which makes them excellent leaders and defenders. The warrior is a nurturer who takes care of those around them, making them feel safe, seen, and respected. They don't put themselves first.

LEAD INCLUSIVELY

A warrior in business understands that inclusivity involves thinking, talking, and engaging all levels of employees. An inclusive leader is transparent and leads by example, someone who not only takes an interest in others' thoughts and ideas but also listens to, acknowledges, and appreciates their perspective. They encourage collaboration in the workplace. They lead and manage people and organizations without biases or prejudices. In an inclusive environment, individuals are treated fairly and feel safe, respected, and valued. Everyone has a sense of *belongingness* and feels encouraged to participate, share their ideas and opinions, and give feedback. In this work environment, everyone thrives.

An inclusive leader also builds up women and minority leaders and is gender inclusive. As an inclusive leader, it is important to recognize and call out any potentially conscious or unconscious gender bias or mindsets that create invisible barriers for women in your organization and in our society. If your goal is to consistently achieve superior business results in retention, productivity, and profitability, then inclusivity is the answer. A warrior in business will cultivate a deep sense of engagement throughout the organization, which is critical for innovation and the bottom line.

An effective business warrior views all genders as equal contributors to the organization and is not afraid to encourage all genders to take on distinct roles and to ensure their skills don't go unnoticed. You must be conscious not to favor one gender over another; you need balance—pay, workload, and expectations all have to be equal. There should be no preferential treatment, but at the same time, you do have to acknowledge that things haven't always been equal and there have been systemic inequalities. This means that for a time, systems and processes may need to be in place to help tip the scales back in the right direction. But at some point, things will need to be equalized.

It is especially important to recognize that women's and men's needs and experiences are different, and to ensure that these differences do not put anyone—women in particular—at a disadvantage. People must have the same opportunities to advance in their careers and be promoted to higher positions. Be a champion in supporting and advancing gender-specific initiatives. Speak up on gender issues, challenge diversity practices, and seek greater representation from diverse groups. In some cases, this may mean creating gender-specific programs for women to bring out their best selves. Mentoring, helping other women in their careers, and ensuring women are more visible are important strategies for promoting gender equality in the workplace.

Our company is certified as a woman-owned and minority-owned business by various agencies and government institutions. We're sometimes approached by larger organizations because they need to get project work done with a woman- or minority-owned business and have a particular partnership percentage to fulfill. In these instances, we always emphasize that we want to be a participating partner and not just meet the project requirement of a woman- or minority-owned business. We want to be engaged in the projects for the right reasons and not just earn money from the project. We've been very intentional in communicating that we do not want to provide our name and certification just to get 10 percent or 20 percent revenue from the project, or just so they can meet the requirement to qualify for the project.

Inclusivity must be cultivated. You must take a close look at long-standing norms, and you must incorporate inclusivity into your everyday life. When you have the right mindset around it, you can build the right systems to empower and develop the skills and experiences of everyone in your organization. In practice, this is not always easy to do, but it's essential. It calls for an authentic, active engagement and willingness to learn. It's not about just putting butts in seats, meeting a quota, or simply saying you're a diverse company. You're looking to actually engage in meaningful ways that bring out the best in others, and it takes steps, systems, and processes that you've put in place to make that happen. Above all, it takes time. Take an interest in your people, invite them to the conversations happening around you, and find out what their skills are. They should know that you value their contribution and need it to sharpen what your company does.

INCLUSIVITY MUST BE CULTIVATED.

Intentionality and inclusivity pave the way for a workplace culture consisting of active, engaged, and motivated people. It requires people to step out of their comfort zones and be courageous enough to express what they want, how they want to grow, what they wish to contribute, and what they want to learn. Build a feeling of trust and create opportunities for people to engage like this. It needs to come from everyone in the company, from the top down, and it must be practiced.

Remember that people are crucial to your business, and you have a responsibility to them. They bring tremendous value to what you do. You could have the best product or service, but at the end of the day, you are still in the business of people. You must give your people the right attention, engagement, and inspiration; not doing so could potentially hurt the organization. Even if some of the principles in this chapter are out of character for you, you can still learn the skills to make all this happen. This is where self-development comes in: To cultivate others, be willing to invest in working on yourself.

A warrior in battle who has set out to accomplish a mission is stronger when they draw from the strengths of all the different people on their team. To be stronger, you need to intentionally include, integrate, develop, and build up your people. To do this effectively, you must ensure you are engaging all of your team—from every background, gender, and cultural context. This kind of inclusivity fortifies your team and sets your entire company up for success. Building up these kinds of diverse and trusting relationships inside and outside of your company will boost your business's resiliency in the long term. Trust and dependability are a solid foundation for growth, innovation, and creativity. Once you have built up those solid relationship foundations, you can inspire your team to explore. Everyone benefits from a good relationship dynamic between skilled and talented team members, and from a diversity of perspectives and experiences. And this ensures the health of your business in the long term.

Executive Summary

- The **foundation of how you lead others** is built on

  1. Your relationships with people

2. How you communicate with them

- When you **invest in the people you work with**, you create a culture where everyone can flourish, and your business can achieve significant success.

- A warrior in business is **dependable, trustworthy, and follows through**.

- A warrior in business is **transparent about shared goals**.

- **Communication is the key** to activating, engaging, and inspiring the people around you.

- The culture of your business is **your company's identity**.

- **The ability to work with diverse cultures** is of the utmost importance to succeed in business today.

- A warrior in business **invites creativity, innovation, and fresh solutions**.

- Warriors take their responsibility to protect others seriously. They are **loyal to their people and organization, standing up for them** and the company's mission.

CHAPTER 9

A WARRIOR IN BUSINESS ALWAYS KNOWS THE NEXT MOVE

———————————————

JUST AS A WARRIOR IN BATTLE PREPARES, strategizes, and battles to gain ground and accomplish a mission, you must do the same in your business and life. The warrior in business knows how to create their own opportunities without leaving things to chance. They are aware that the perfect time may never come or may come too late. They understand how to seize the moment, and they recognize that spending time on the wrong things or being too slow to take action can cost them. They're always thinking about how to transform and accelerate their company's growth and expansion, and they stay focused on the next move.

Once a warrior has gone through preparation, planning, and training, the moves become second nature. Similarly, warriors in business draw on their skills and experience to know where to focus their efforts and resources. They are focused, decisive, aware, and understand responsibility and accountability. They have mental toughness with a purpose and goal in mind, leading them to think rationally and draw sensible conclusions to outmaneuver their competition.

When you have cultivated the mindset of a warrior, you will have the presence of mind to know when to act, how to overcome the obstacles and difficulties before you, and how to capitalize on the opportunities that present themselves. You'll know the next move and be able to proceed forward with tenacity and resilience, conquering the day and achieving your desired outcome.

Chess is often used as a metaphor for planning your next moves in business, war, or life. It presents a deep intellectual challenge that has many advantages, not only for your mind but also for your enterprise. In a game of chess, you learn to anticipate your rival's next move. You must not only quickly recognize your own strengths and weaknesses but those of your opponent as well. Chess is, in many ways, a SWOT analysis. It teaches you that just like in life, every decision you make can result in either an advantage or a disadvantage. Even acting upon your shrewdest decision can yield an adverse outcome.

WHAT OTHERS DO IS OUTSIDE YOUR CONTROL.

In chess, the pieces must keep on moving until there is a victory. This is much like the life of a business warrior: You must keep moving strategically until you have reached your goal. You can't depend on your opponent or rival to make a bad move before you make a good one. What others do is outside your control. Chess players know that much like life, the game consists of a limited number of moves. A trained player calculates and takes the right move from the start. To be resilient in business, you need to have a similar mindset.

There was a study that examined the effect of chess training on the academic performance in various courses of middle school children in rural India.[6] The sample consisted of one hundred students in sixth grade, with an intervention group undergoing chess training and a control group. The results of the paired samples t-test analysis (the procedure computes the differences between values of the two variables for each case) showed significant improvement in the academic performances of students in English, social studies, and science after a year of training in chess skills.

When we were growing up in the sixties and seventies, there were no computers, smartphones, or social media sites. For much of our childhood and teen years, we played chess or bridge a lot to entertain ourselves, and it was a household game. Through chess we learned how to strategize, become problem-solvers, and analyze critical skills, all of which became second nature to us through practice. The skills we acquired through chess and bridge helped shape our later approach to strategy in our business, strengthened our intellectual abilities, and improved our cognitive skills. They also gave us the competence to respond to changes in our business environment and use our critical thinking skills.

- - - - - - - - - - -

6   E. Joseph, S. Manharan, Veena Easvaradoss, David Chandran, "A Study on the Impact of Chess Training on Creativity of Indian School Children," Cognitive Sciences Society annual meeting white paper, 2017, https://www.semanticscholar.org/paper/A-Study-on-the-Impact-of-Chess-Training-on-of-Joseph-Manoharan/4b13f637908b48e654044b4beec0fd336abbb6fb.

IF YOU MAKE THE WRONG MOVE, YOU CAN'T EXPECT TO WIN.

Whether you play chess or not, you must develop the ability to perform a type of SWOT analysis of your own business if you hope to achieve success. Without critical thinking about the circumstances before you and careful anticipation of what's to come, you'll have a tough time knowing your next move. If you make the wrong move, you can't expect to win.

RUN A MENTAL CHECKLIST BEFORE EACH MOVE

Before deciding on the right move, a warrior in business must first prepare their mind, going through a mental checklist—essentially a disciplined list of thoughts. This mental checklist allows them to engage in an internal dialogue with themselves, helping them envision their steps in advance. It enables them to think critically about what's ahead and make a wise and informed decision about how to proceed. This mental preparation often relies on research, tangible data, and feedback they've received from others. This is the moment when all the preparation, planning, and training comes into play. The warrior benefits from and is strengthened by all this preparation, and as a result, they can effectively determine their next move. As a warrior becomes increasingly mature and experienced, a written list is not needed before each move, because they've trained themselves to ask the questions in their mind.

The moves you plan for tend to fall into one of three categories. The first is when you've prepared fully and adequately and have enough foreknowledge to inform your next move. You're aware of the situation to the extent you can be, understand the facts at hand, and have the time you need to think through your move—even coming up with contingencies and alternate plans. An example of this situation may be where you are launching a new product or service—you have done a lot of market research; gathered data, facts, and figures; and you are able to gauge and evaluate how everything will turn out.

With the war in Ukraine, before Russian troops crossed the Ukrainian border to invade, there was massive movement of armored vehicles and other red flags months before the war began. So, Ukraine and its allies around the world had foreknowledge of what was transpiring. They did not know the exact date it would take place, but they understood that war was imminent. Allied forces, including the USA, began to offer assistance and intelligence, allowing for some level of advance preparation because of that foreknowledge. Preparation comes after knowledge, but both are factors considered by military leaders and governments.

The second category is when a warrior needs to walk into circumstances that are unpredictable and unknown. You have time to plan your move, but there's much less predictability. Due to the uncertainty in this kind of situation, people are unable to fully prepare. But nonetheless, they have to make a move, so they must do their best and decide on the right one to take. Whether you start a business, launch a new product or service, make changes to your existing line, decide to move your business to another location, or choose to hire a new employee, there will always be some percentage of uncertainty. In these instances, don't waste a lot of time pondering what to do. Be fully present and attentive. Create your mental checklist. Think critically about the situation, as a chess player might. Pull in trusted consultants from outside your organization for their feedback. It's great to have the facts and hard data. But overall, you will be at a better advantage if you have a strong, optimistically charged mindset.

Consider the launch of the Apollo mission. This voyage to the moon inspired people across the USA and around the world to dream about the impossible. It gave us a whole new outlook on life. The Apollo landing on the moon was one of the most miraculous entrepreneurial endeavors in the history of the USA and the world at the time. As with any good business plan, the minds working at NASA and behind Apollo were also able to visualize possible "what-if" scenarios and plan for potential situations that may or may not occur during a mission. In this way, they developed contingency plans to overcome each situation that might potentially occur. We as entrepreneurs, in a different sense, also prepare to launch our projects to the "moon," to see what we can achieve and find out if our preparation and knowledge have put us in position to reach our goal.

Thinking outside the box may not work all the time. Leaders at NASA realized that thinking within its own box—by empowering its internal resources, building on its knowledge, and adding additional creativity and training—was the correct way forward. In your own business, think of resources that already exist inside the box of your company, adding innovative ideas as you go along, as this may be the correct way to proceed.

MORE MINDS CAN OFTEN BE BETTER THAN ONE.

As with any endeavor, we need to presume that failure may occur. Not all of NASA's missions ended in success or were without enormous challenges. But NASA reviewed the causes of the setbacks in each case, inviting external experts to help determine any weaknesses and then drafting innovative solutions. In so doing, NASA demonstrated that you don't have to be shy or feel small in seeking outside help and guidance. More minds can often be better than one.

A warrior in business doesn't spend time beating themselves up for a move they didn't make or a move they made that failed. They don't hold others responsible for the circumstances, thinking about all they lost or could lose, or asking themselves, "Why did this happen to me?" They don't let the problem cause them to lack self-confidence. Letting go of self-doubt drives a warrior to think objectively and move forward. If something was not in your plans, accept, modify, and adopt a new plan and move on.

The third category is when you have to make a fast, immediate decision. Such a moment requires 100 percent of your attention. Your advanced preparation will allow you to focus fully and perform at your best in these moments, even if perfect accuracy may not be guaranteed. Quickly assess the situation, remove anything irrelevant from the equation, take a leap of faith, and decide on the appropriate action.

Making decisions quickly is often easier for small-to-midsize businesses, which tend to be able to move more nimbly. However, this ability to pivot quickly may also come with a higher risk at times. With large organizations, on the other hand, decision-making tends to take longer, as they are often weighed down by their own size, systems, processes, and bureaucracy. Exceptionally large corporations can be especially slow to make changes when needed. In the seventies, US automakers had no defense when Japanese carmakers started flooding the American market with new cars. The US carmakers took a long time to react, and by that time, the Japanese manufacturers had captured a competitive advantage, largely due to their cars' quality and price, and US automakers lost much of their existing market share.

If you've trained your mind in the way of a business warrior, you'll have the ability to respond rather than react, operating from a place of mental and emotional resiliency, so you can feel more confident that you'll be okay, whatever decision you make. You increase your odds of making a good decision when you have the warrior mindset. Regardless, make a move. No move you make is going to be fail-safe. It's still possible to miscalculate or end up making a mistake. But learn to move on from these moments, viewing mistakes as opportunities to gain experience and improve. Even the most successful business leaders make the wrong move from time to time. Life is too short to regret what you did in the past, and there's plenty more you can do today to drive a different outcome for the future. Don't worry about things you can't change. When a moment has passed, accept it, use it to gain experience, decide to come out better on the other side, and move on.

ACCELERATE THE GROWTH OF YOUR COMPANY

A warrior in business sees the big picture and thinks well ahead. Whether you are going through a crisis or not, recognizing growth and expansion opportunities for your company and quickly making the right decisions to implement them can go a long way in leveraging how you can use the time, resources, and situations that you are in. Keep the end goal in sight and look at your circumstances through a strategic lens.

Strategy is a way of viewing situations that helps to steer your reactions to changes in events. The faster your reactions, the more likely you will succeed. Whether in war or in business, can you always plan your moves? No, but you can have a strategy about how to move when you face an opponent or confront a situation that calls for action. Allow these strategies to direct your actions toward your end goal. Work with a plan A, but also have a plan B and a plan C to fall back on. It is essential to have a contingency plan to account for any unknowns. Small-to-midsize businesses are often especially reluctant to have multiple plans. But businesses with adequate plans can react faster when disruptions occur. With a backup plan, your recovery from such unexpected events can be very quick.

Think critically through the different scenarios before you and acknowledge the unexpected things that could happen. If you can anticipate some of these situations and put a plan in place around them, then you can begin to manage them sooner. This may entail coming up with a mental or written checklist for the various scenarios. Think well ahead about having a strategy in place. A victorious army first wins and then seeks battle, but a defeated army first battles and then seeks victory. This is the difference between those with strategy and those without forethoughts. If you do the necessary work ahead of time, already establishing the mindset of a warrior, you are at an advantage before the battle even begins. Once there, you're better equipped to face the challenges and make the right moves in the moment.

Be decisive, take calculated risks, and expect to make sacrifices. These are the things a warrior in business must be willing to do if they want to succeed in battle and expand their territory. It's a tough and competitive climate out there. If you want to grow and expand your organization, anticipate the work you'll need to do up front and in the heat of battle. You must demonstrate determination and commitment to your goals because every step you take will bring you closer to your mission's goal.

PRACTICE EVOLUTION AND INNOVATION

Businesses must evolve. When we look back at where we started, we can see how we've evolved. Nip left the corporate world to begin our venture, and Rita started with an accounting and tax practice.

BUSINESSES MUST EVOLVE.

Nip's consultancy evolves as he constantly adapts to the ever-changing business environment and markets. He continuously makes an effort to give in-depth strategic direction to clients doing business not only in the US but also in other parts of the world. He leans on his consulting skills and his experience gained from collaborating with diverse clients to bring fresh ideas to our clientele on growth strategies, cost reduction, minimizing scrap, improving process design, and new market development for products and services.

Rita's role has evolved as well. She was never totally happy just doing accounting and taxes. She realized early on that businesses need much more than just basic accounting. So, she became a strategic partner, especially for small-to-midsize businesses. Alongside other team members, she was driven to create financially sound businesses by focusing on their cash flow and placing emphasis on financial management, operations, business plans, marketing plans, strategic plans, market research, branding, coaching, and leadership training, all of which give businesses the power to grow and thrive.

What we are doing now looks nothing like what we had started initially, but that's because we chose to make moves that kept us growing, learning, building our skill sets, and finding new ways to deliver value to people. Over the years, we've learned new things, discovered what we love to do (and what we don't), found a niche, and adjusted our offerings to better meet the needs of our customers and our lives. We've also engaged in the process of self-development, improving ourselves along the way. While the growth process was challenging and sometimes emotionally and financially difficult, it was worth it in every way. We now work in a way that's aligned with our values, doing something that inspires us and allows us to be a strategic partner in the growth and development of each one of our clients.

Learning and growing both emphasize the need to evolve in business. Because our needs are changing and the needs of our clients change as well, we recognized that the right move was to adjust and grow. If we had stayed where we were on our first day of business, we probably wouldn't still be in business today. We guesstimate that many of the businesses in the USA go under because they are reluctant to change with the times or are too slow to evolve. In recent history, we saw how Apple not only found innovative ways to change with the times but also came to define the times through its innovations. The iPod, iPhone, iPad, and other inventions were the first of their kind, and Apple became a leader in tech and innovation. Your small business needs to follow their example by working hard and applying innovations and technology to stay ahead in your industry.

IT IS EITHER DO OR DIE. WE CANNOT REMAIN STATIC.

Whether you are the Apple of your industry or you are a small business, when you embrace change, you foster creativity and innovative ideas that allow you to stay ahead of the competition and grow your business.

It takes time, effort, and money to evolve and grow a business, but we can speak from experience when we say that the outcomes are always worth it. Ask yourself, How has my business evolved over the years? In today's competitive markets, innovation is no longer a choice. It is either do or die. We cannot remain static. Even if you want to remain stable and get to a point where you feel comfortable with your business, coasting still requires many changes. Nothing in life is stable; either you go up or down.

Innovation means introducing new ideas into your processes, systems, products, and services that allow you to improve your business and serve your clients better. And yes, *innovation* can sometimes be a scary word for small-to-midsize business owners. But innovation doesn't have to mean sending a rocket to the south side of the moon—it might be something small. Innovation is what allows you to grow and move forward. It might encompass something as simple as a process improvement. It's more doable than you might think. If a certain task takes you three hours, how might you reduce it to two hours? Can you cut the cost of something for better profitability? Do you need to adapt to a new platform so your business can innovate or stay competitive in the market?

One simple example from our own business is the automated clearing house (ACH) platform, an electronic funds transfer system that facilitates payments in the USA and internationally. This system allows for receiving and sending payments and can help businesses improve their cash flow. It was designed to create more efficiency and speed in the process, offer security, and be more cost effective in the long run than the manual system for issuing and receiving checks. All these benefits serve to strengthen fluidity and the bottom line because cash flows in and out of the business more efficiently. Especially for small or developing companies, it can be faster and easier to manage, and it can reduce costs. Many years back, when we automated our system and chose the ACH platform for our business, we saw a tremendous improvement in our cash flow.

Any of these continual and gradual changes to improve processes and systems are what innovation looks like on a smaller scale. That doesn't make them any less meaningful. People in small-to-midsize businesses need to continue to make things work better. That's how you survive. That's how you move forward. That's how you innovate and change, and that is how you increase profitability. Sometimes, your next move needs to be about making a change or improvement to your systems or processes. Welcome that and view it as a way to strengthen and fortify yourself in the competitive business climate where everything seems like a battle.

It's important to take the time to step back from the everyday practices of your business and think about things at a higher level. You don't want to get stuck in the routine tasks around operations, unable to recognize when they're no longer serving you well. Small innovations can improve efficiency, profitability, and service. You also create more ease for your clients, and they will love it. A warrior in business knows that to be strong on the battlefield, they need to do this behind the scenes.

You must focus on business transformation, changing your mindset and being open to change. If you want to create an impact, you need to think beyond the four walls of your business. You must experiment with new ideas. Surround yourself with a team of people with bold and brave ideas, who are innovators, entrepreneurs, intrapreneurs, go-getters, and changemakers. Find product designers who have the courage to challenge the conventional way of thinking about sustainability and who offer inspiration and ideas on how to make it work. Business warriors are enthusiastic about generating innovative ideas. They are not just focused on money. They tend to care more about the influence and the impact that their products and services have on humanity. Understanding why innovation is important is key, and how we can encourage it in the workplace can be transformative.

No doubt you have observed the recent massive disruptions to businesses around the world because of COVID. It forced business owners to change the way they did things and to be innovative. Those who were willing to adapt and change to the new norm made tremendous progress. Whether it was moving to a remote working environment or limiting the number of people who could enter, businesses found ways to adapt. Business leaders must constantly look for new ways and be on the lookout for groundbreaking ideas because you can't easily solve new problems with old solutions. Innovation is necessary for businesses to modify, adapt, and defeat the challenges of change. You can become sluggish and stagnant if you are just doing things the way you've previously done them. You need to constantly evolve and stay relevant. As a business owner, you need to always explore and identify what opportunities the market offers. Warriors in business are always improving how they reach their prospects and clients, experimenting with innovative experiences, and banking on data-driven strategies to confront any challenges. The outcome is a stronger, more agile organization that's always on the lookout for new ways to do things.

Innovation fosters growth. Lack of progress can be extremely harmful to your business. Achieving organizational and economic growth through innovation is key to staying ahead of your competition. Innovation will separate you from your competition and distinguish your business from others.

Warriors in business are constantly evaluating where they are now and where they are going. They know how to transform themselves from bricklayers into organizational architects. They chalk out the strategic vision for their people and organization. To have a warrior's mindset, you must be clear on your purpose. If you are set to achieve greater things, you must find your way to get there. A warrior breaks through the preconceptions. Once you know your purpose, you are on the path to moving forward with more clarity and focus, you know who you are, and you become more enthusiastic about your goals.

INNOVATION FOSTERS GROWTH.

Bringing change is always challenging. Change affects all of us, whether we are a mega corporation or a small business. There will be resistance, roadblocks, and rejections, and as human beings, we all tend to be averse to change. It is the responsibility of a business warrior to help people recognize that change brings new opportunities. Then it is easier to collectively understand and adapt to change. You cannot forget that change is the answer to any crisis in business. When business as a routine is unworkable, your methods and even services and products may need innovation.

We saw many examples of this during the COVID pandemic. Hospitals, retail shops, grocery stores, restaurants, and delivery services implemented new standards and practices and are continuing to build and improve them as situations evolve. We witnessed new protocols around safety, observed more outdoor spaces, and adapted to innovative technologies in restaurants and venues. Adversity forced us to think of new ways of doing business, adapting to needs, and serving customers. Though these were and continue to be incredibly challenging times, innovations have grown out of these, with companies coming up with new ways of doing things that became not simply great selling points but things that genuinely helped improve people's lives.

To manage change driven by innovation, a business warrior must do the following:

- Define the purpose.

- Have clear and consistent communication.

- Appoint change leaders.

- Train and educate.

- Execute the change.

INNOVATE AND MANAGE CHANGE

A warrior in business creates and follows a plan that is sustainable. Here the term "sustainability" refers also to business resources. Sustainability is when our business, partners, allies, and the communities where we operate will thrive for generations to come—but only if the multitudes of people who contribute to our success thrive as well.

Sustainability can also mean self-development and the development of your employees. Many resources go into training an employee, whether it be on the job or in a classroom. Retention itself is part of sustainability because if that employee leaves, you have just wasted all those resources used in the training. So, the training of these employees becomes a resource, and that resource will be thrown away if it is not successful in terms of retention.

BE A TORCHBEARER.

In business, sustainability looks like maintaining a plan. It's a conscious effort that requires a substantial investment of time and money. If you feel strongly about an issue and you think it can also benefit our society at large, pursue it. Be a torchbearer. Become an encouraging voice of advocacy beyond the boundaries of your business and blaze trails by creating value for employees, consumers, and the public. The visionary thinking and passion behind your business sustainability plan will be memorialized for years to come.

In manufacturing—of any product or even service—the process is documented to show how the parts are developed. We define this in an earlier chapter as "man, material, and machine." Everything is captured, so the system can continue even as man, material, or machine changes or improves. This runs parallel to sustainability. Defining the process in your business allows you to be sustainable and to use your available resources well as things change over time.

To be sustainable, businesses need to have systems and processes in place. When you think about processes, you may always think about manufacturing and large businesses. But every business step has a process, and it can always be improved. For example, in our own business, we have noticed that creating a purchase order (PO) has many steps, as in most organizations. There are steps that must take place even before the PO is written. We have a requirement, and we know which supplier can produce it. We get competitive quotations, and somebody must review all those competitive quotations, look at their quality reputation, and decide if the supplier is going to be adequate for our purpose at this moment. Now the PO has to be written. In many corporations, this can take from two days to two months because the order must go from one desk to another and another to get signatures. And a person who needs to sign might have fourteen thousand other things they need to do. So it takes a few days.

Nip walked through these steps at one of the plants he worked with, observing that 98 percent of the time it took to issue a PO was simply waiting time. So he decided that one PO gets a green tag, the next PO gets a red tag, and so on. This new ad-hoc process created the priority for the PO to move from one signatory to the next. Even in a small business, it may take a few days to two or three weeks to write a PO, as it goes from computer to computer to computer. And even in a small business like ours, when a proper PO is written, even if Nip has to write it himself, it may take three days because suddenly something else comes up that takes priority, and the PO gets bumped. You need to look at the steps and then determine if you're wasting your own internal resources and how you can streamline for greater sustainability.

CULTIVATE RESILIENCE

A warrior in business cultivates resilience. Resilience must be intentional. What does resilience in business look like? It includes the organization's ability to recognize stress, preserve critical operations during a high-risk event, adjust its focus and priorities, know how to navigate through disruption, and evolve and grow to nurture a warrior mind for itself and its teams.

Resilience is when you are focused, determined, decisive, and have an unwavering courage to take a step forward in the face of adversity. Your role as leader of your organization goes beyond guiding your teams to meet goals. Cultivating resilience requires giving guidance and support to your people—especially those who are struggling with fear and a victim attitude—to inspire and empower them, so they are not afraid and are equipped with tools and resources to have the courage to move. You set the example by personifying these principles in your actions and decisions.

Before you think of cultivating resilience in others, you need to be resilient yourself.

- Find your sense of purpose. With a defined purpose, one remains motivated and you won't get discouraged as you face demanding situations.

- Believe in yourself and in your abilities. This can help you bounce back during the many crises you may face during various life cycles of your business.

- Surround yourself with positive people.

- Have a strong social and professional network.

- Act. Don't wait for problems to disappear. Take steps toward making your situation better and less stressful. Focus on the progress that you have made thus far and on planning your next steps.

EXPAND YOUR INFLUENCE

A warrior expands their influence. Their reputation precedes them. Companies live and die by the leadership abilities of their executives and leaders. Of all the things that are required for a business to succeed, we place leadership at the top of the list. Let's talk about how a warrior in business can expand their influence, not just by showing their competence and strength. They take a different approach. First of all, they are connected to themselves. Second, they know how to connect with others.

When you are connected to yourself, you know who you are and what you want to be about. If you know how to connect with others, this allows you to influence them with your ideas and motivate them to act. Connecting with others ensures follow-ups, deepens conversations, and takes ideas to the next step. Your people will trust you and look up to you as a leader who they believe has their back and is calm, clearheaded, and courageous. You will earnestly create a feeling of warmth among your people.

We at S&A don't advertise much. Our clients come to us for our name—our reputation, prior work, service to others, and integrity. How do you expand your influence? It's not just by expanding your advertising dollars. We did it not just by showing up but also by participating in, connecting with, and engaging with others. We've built deep relationships with people in our circles of influence and offered impeccable service, and this is what our reputation came to be built on.

YOU MUST DELIVER WHAT YOU PROMISE.

We all live and work in an increasingly transparent world. When you make promises and commitments, you must deliver and honor them. It is your relationship with every prospect, customer, employee, and stakeholder that will make or break your reputation. It is about being authentic and walking the talk and talking the walk. When you own your own business, your business is an extension of who you are as a person. Are you a person who is honest, dependable, and keeps your word? These qualities can have a bearing on how much confidence others place in you. You must deliver what you promise.

It takes commitment, hard work, and diligence to build a strong, positive reputation, and maintaining that reputation takes continuous effort. Compelling reputations are built up over a span of years, but sometimes it can take only a few seconds to ruin them. Losing is extremely easy. So, it is an ongoing process to nurture and protect your reputation. The best way to gain and protect your reputation is to run your business with honesty and the highest integrity.

Whether you are playing chess, starting a business, or landing on the moon, a resilient mind is what sets the warrior in business apart and equips them with what they need to accomplish even seemingly impossible tasks. The mindset that's needed is developed in advance of the battle and serves as a source of strength and inspiration. To win the battle and rise above your enemies, think in terms of evolution and innovation for your products and services and rely on the warrior attributes you've learned throughout this book, including your ability to assess a situation quickly, remain focused on your mission, and fight alongside others as a team player. Not everything in the battle will go your way, but it is the process of fighting—not the goal, personal achievement, or outcome—that makes an effective warrior. Embrace change as you cross new terrains, learn to cope with the unknown, and expect to think on your feet. In business, there are no certainties, but mental preparation, planning, and the honing of your strengths as a warrior will ready you for the next move, whether planned or unplanned.

Executive Summary

- **Before deciding on the right move**, a warrior in business must first prepare their mind with a disciplined list of thoughts.

- There are **three scenarios** you must prepare for in business: when you are able **to fully prepare for a decision**, when you have **plenty of time to decide** but there are unknown variables, and when you have mere **seconds to decide**.

- If you've trained your mind in the way of a business warrior, you'll have the ability to **respond rather than react** when the time comes to make the right decision.

- It is essential to **have a contingency plan** to speed up your recovery time in the face of unforeseen challenges.

- Innovation means **introducing new ideas** into your processes, systems, products, and services that allow you to improve your business and serve your clients better.

- **Change and innovation are the answer** to any crisis in business.

- All businesses need to have systems and processes in place **to be sustainable**.

- The best way to **gain and protect your reputation** is to run your business with honesty and integrity.

- **A resilient mind is what sets the warrior in business apart** and equips them with what they need to accomplish even the most challenging tasks.

LEADING LIKE AN EVERYDAY WARRIOR

YOU'VE JUST FINISHED READING THIS BOOK AND now carry in your mind all the concepts we have shared: tools earned through years of lived experience; professional challenges; and consistent, mindful efforts to reframe and refine our mindsets as business warriors. You have everything you need to cultivate the mental agility for ensuring your business's success in the future. It's up to you to take the next steps and apply the teachings in this book to your own life and business by embracing the warrior's character, drive, and strategy. Now is the time to lead, and we are challenging you to do more. You must commit yourself to acting and pushing yourself outside your comfort zone, or risk failure. Only then can you truly begin to make preparations to ensure future victory.

Now that you know what you must do, you might be wondering, *Where and how do I begin?* We suggest you start by assessing where you are in your journey and what battles you are facing. To lead others, you must first lead yourself, and to lead yourself, you must know the landscape before you and where you are headed within it. Once you've established the challenges and opportunities facing you, move on to whichever lessons will best serve what your business needs now: Tend to your relationships, identify and embrace disruption, prepare for your opponent's next move, and plan for future growth. As you begin integrating the wisdom contained in this book into the way you approach business, you will find yourself working better and smarter, building more meaningful relationships with others, and not only persevering but also remaining unbeaten in the face of adversity. **You will become a leader who is resilient, confident, and courageous—a leader who leads fearlessly.**

Being a warrior is a way of life. We all encounter tough times, and that is as true in business as it is in our personal lives. A warrior is someone who is prepared for adversity because they have put in the time to develop the skills and mindset they need to succeed *before* things get tough. Warriors may enjoy peaceful lives, but they never forget that unforeseen challenges, attacks, or disruption may be just around the corner. In the face of that adversity, the business warrior rises to the challenge and leads. Take the next step with a warrior's spirit, be a leader, and start a dialogue with your network. Together, we can shape how all our institutions learn and grow.

There's never a point at which you will achieve perfect leadership. Leading isn't about being right all the time or having all the answers. You will face many setbacks and failures, but the mental agility you have gained by following the teachings in this book will help you adapt to changing situations and will guide you in overcoming adversity. A warrior in business is prepared for and expects ongoing growth, professionally and personally. They understand they're constantly evolving and always learning. A warrior puts their ego aside to serve in the best interests of others. They approach each day with an open mind and enter every battle anticipating that they're not going to fight perfectly. Being a leader isn't a fixed or static condition. It's a state of mind—a continuous openness to improving, developing, learning, growing, and practicing. Evolution means you must expect change and commit yourself to the mindset that you will survive, adapt, and become more relevant in the new landscape you find yourself in.

Every one of us is a warrior. Though you may not feel like a warrior every day, the warrior spirit resides within us all. You just need to look inside yourself to discover the warrior spirit—your authentic self. It is a voice deep within you that lets you take action and persevere through unthinkable odds. With a warrior spirit, you will not need to fear facing down undefeatable probabilities, because you realize that you will learn from your failures. You will never quit when things are difficult, because you understand that your deepest strength lies in your resilience. A warrior is driven by what is possible. When life knocks you down, if nothing else works, turning to your faith and your inner belief can give you the strength to power through adversity and pain.

If on your warrior's journey you find that you need our guidance, advice, and coaching to help navigate through your business's ups and downs, then remember, **you can always lean on us.**

We feel confident that this book contains timeless, hard-earned wisdom and practices that will continue to serve business leaders as a source of evergreen inspiration, insight, and action-oriented introspection for generations of readers to come. Proudly, we share this book with our readers, not only to have as a roadmap for their business, but also to give them access to our consultants' combined 400-plus years of invaluable collective experience in global operations, organizational effectiveness, and development and thought leadership.

We passionately believe that our long hours of research, writing, rewriting—of blood, sweat, and tears—will outlive us, and that these words will find a place of honor in the lives and libraries of future business leaders until our great-grandchildren are walking the earth.

ACKNOWLEDGMENTS

WE CARRY IN OUR HEARTS THE EXTRAORDINARY gratitude for so many people whose love, support, and guidance have given us the courage to write this book. Without naming each one of them, we have taken a collective approach to recognize all the influencers in life who have provided us with some form of spiritual, emotional, moral, and financial support while undertaking the challenge of authoring a book.

To Higher Power—We bow to His/Her grace, who continues to guide us with the many blessings to live our life with courage and wisdom.

To our parents—You raised us with good values and gave us the encouragement and best education to be lifelong learners.

To our children and grandchildren—You are a source of unending strength, the reason we smile, the reason we laugh, and the reason we keep going and look forward to every day with hope and inspiration.

To our extended family—Your constant encouragement, love, support, guidance, blessings, and prayers give us the strength to go through life's challenges with determination and without fear.

To our friends—Your presence, the joyful moments we have shared together over the years, and the fellowship of being there for each other have made us strong to lead with endurance.

To our clients—Your trust, faith in our abilities, and above all your business constantly make us give our **absolute best** in every endeavor we undertake.

To our community—Our collaborations, resources, alliances, and partnerships we have built together have become an integral part of our life, to live in, work in, and serve.

To our people—We are grateful to all of our consultants here at home and around the globe for your devotion, hard work, and integrity, and for making our business and life so meaningful.

To our countries—India, where we were born and raised with deep values, and the USA, where we live today, which provides us with the countless opportunities to be successful.

A very special thanks to our two daughters Kavita Vazirani and Anjulika Saini, who are the source of our strength and inspiration.

With Immense Gratitude,
Nip and Rita Singh

ABOUT THE AUTHORS

NIPENDRA "NIP" SINGH *has decades of knowledge*, deep understanding, and experience in the high-technology manufacturing business, primarily in aircraft engine components. He has consulted over the past thirty years for companies in North America, Europe, and Asia. He has spearheaded major updates of existing and new manufacturing plants in the aerospace, automotive, and commercial casting sectors. He has assisted companies worldwide to develop new business process models to innovate and promote technologies and related products to expand their market share.

Nip leads as the cofounder, chairman, and CEO of S&A Consulting Group, a global resource management consulting company. He previously served in various high-level managerial capacities for major players in the aerospace industry, including Rolls-Royce, GE Engines, TRW Corporation, and Precision Castparts Corporation.

He is actively involved in and devoted to the Investment Casting Institute (ICI) of America and has been a board member for the last thirty-plus years, serving on numerous committees and is currently serving as president of the board of directors. Nip has been a key presenter at numerous regional and world conferences. Nip's vision and thought leadership helped make S&A Consulting Group a worldwide leader in manufacturing technology consulting.

Photographer credit Bruce S. Ford

RITA N. SINGH *is the inspiring authority* on entrepreneurship and leadership development. Rita is a forward-thinking, visionary executive leader with strategic acumen, offering more than thirty years of progressive management achievements across multiple industries, ranging from closely held family businesses to midsize and large businesses. Rita has been recognized locally, regionally, and internationally for her business innovation and leadership. As an executive coach, she focuses on helping business executives to become better business leaders. Rita works with individuals and business owners to develop skills in entrepreneurial leadership at various levels of their career through an ongoing curriculum, individual coaching sessions, workshops, seminars, lecture series, forums, and conferences. She has excelled as an expert entrepreneur, brilliant executive coach, changemaker, leadership strategist, dynamic speaker, author and moderator, mentor, philanthropist, thought leader, consultant, and CPA.

Rita serves as cofounder with her husband, Nip Singh, of S&A Consulting Group, a global resource management consulting company, and CEO and founder of Elite Women Around the World˚. She scales her impact by leading an organization that advises and coaches CEOs, executives, and emerging leaders in major corporations, political arenas, nonprofits, and entrepreneurial ventures. She is the recipient of numerous national and international awards, recognitions, and accolades.

GET IN TOUCH

Consulting Group LLP

Nipendra "Nip" Singh
Cofounder, Chairman, and Chief Executive Officer
NSingh@SA-ConsultingGroup.com

Rita N. Singh, EMBA, MA, CPA
Cofounder, Chief Financial and Operations Officer
RSingh@SA-ConsultingGroup.com

https://sa-consultinggroup.com
Info@SA-ConsultingGroup.com